TORN
TOGETHER

ONE FAMILY'S JOURNEY THROUGH ADDICTION, TREATMENT, & THE RESTAURANT INDUSTRY.

SHAAREN PINE & SCOTT MAGNUSON

authorHOUSE®

AuthorHouse™
1663 Liberty Drive
Bloomington, IN 47403
www.authorhouse.com
Phone: 1 (800) 839-8640

Published by AuthorHouse 02/11/2015

ISBN: 978-1-4969-6584-4 (sc)
ISBN: 978-1-4969-6585-1 (hc)
ISBN: 978-1-4969-6583-7 (e)

This book is dedicated to all the families who still suffer.
We write for you.

A portion of the proceeds from the sale of *Torn Together* will go to support our non-profit, Restaurant Recovery™. Restaurant Recovery provides comprehensive solutions to address addiction and its effects on restaurant employees, their families and the restaurant industry.

Restaurant Recovery helps restaurant workers find and pay for drug and alcohol treatment, and helps loved ones get the assistance they need. Creating support networks, Restaurant Recovery is devoted to the continuing care of restaurant workers who are struggling with addiction, seeking sobriety or are in recovery. Restaurant Recovery advocates for change in the restaurant industry through increased awareness of its unique culture

ACKNOWLEDGEMENTS

We'd like to thank our daughter, Ara, for her patience and strength. You are an amazing human being, and we love you so much.

Thank you to:

    Richard Rashke for being willing to read our first draft and encouraging us to share our story.

    Paula Kaufmann for editing and helping us to delve deeper.

    Tim Krepp for answering lots of book-related questions and writing some H Street history for us.

    Jan Haskell-Mohr for her editing skills.

    Elise Bernard for letting us use two of her photos.

    The Argo Crew for being such a great team.

And so many thanks to our wonderful neighborhood for being so supportive of us, both personally and professionally, for forgiving our failures, and believing in us.

Shaaren: I'd like to thank @higher_powered, Dave B (@funguydave), @ashleydex, Jean from @unpickledblog, B from thesexaddicts.wordpress.com, @bobby_steps, and the rest of the #xa crew for helping me through it. One day at a time. My eternal love to the adult adoptee community for helping me reclaim my voice. And, thanks to Lois W for paving the way for the families.

Scott: I'd like to thank my wife, Shaaren, for sticking in there with me. And also the people at BHOPB and Kolmac for breaking me down and building me up. Thanks to Joe Englert and Cheryl Webb for not giving up on me or the Argonaut. Thanks to Howard Yoon for letting me pick his brain about the publishing world. Endless gratitude to Noah Levine for his inspirational, life-changing story. And, of course, to Bill W for starting the recovery movement.

Note: There may be things in this book that are difficult to read (for those touched by addiction *and* for those who haven't been). We hope that in sharing our story, we may help others who are struggling.

Also, we are not experts in addiction, treatment, or recovery. We only speak about our own lives and experiences. Sometimes, we make sweeping generalizations, but these generalizations are based only on our experiences. We do not speak for all addicts or all loved ones. We don't believe that all addicts are entirely the same, and we do not believe that there is one treatment that will always work best.

We have indicated all places where names have been changed.

CHAPTER 1

Scott & Shaaren

Scott

I should have been happy—we had successfully reopened the Argonaut after the fire and business was better than expected. But being constantly hung over, needing drugs just to function, and working so hard to hide everything about my addiction, made me extremely irritable. Shaaren couldn't figure out why I was getting so belligerent. Of course, I was *supposed* to be sober and it didn't make sense as to why I was getting worse. And in response, she had started trying to control my poor behavior, all of which made me very defensive and angry. The more I tried to cover up everything, the angrier I got.

I began to pick fights with just about everyone: staff, customers, and especially Shaaren. I had become an asshole, a monster. I was full of rage. No one knew the extent of my disease, not even me—especially not me. I was so unhappy. But I hid all my thoughts and emotions from everyone. I simply closed off the world. I had lost most of the friends I used to have and was working hard to push away the few who remained, including Shaaren. At the same time, I complained constantly about not having any friends and I blamed my wife for it.

Shaaren

* * * *

April 12, 2011—Despair. Most of the year I was carried through by the love we received after the fire, but here we are, back to regular life, and I'm failing miserably.

I'm angry. And AH [program speak for Alcoholic Husband], is worse than he was a year ago. I wanted (a month ago) to believe that things were getting worse because they were on their way to getting better. But now I'm not so sure.

He's mean all the time. His actions seem only to be based on spite. He's unreliable and untrustworthy. But of course he is, right? He's an addict and an alcoholic!

I'm sad. I feel like crying all the time. I'm tired. I feel like Ara is the only light in my life. I want a partner. I want a husband. I want somebody I can count on. If it weren't for his issues of addiction, I swear, there would be very few issues in our marriage. Almost none, in fact. And I know that sounds ridiculous....But it's true!

I just want him to choose me! I want him to choose us! To see that we're worth it. That what he'll be gaining with us is so much better than what he'd be giving up by not using.

I want to be chosen. I want to be loved. And appreciated. I want to be with somebody who wants to be with me! I want to not have somebody feel contempt for me!

And even as I write this, I wonder what the answer is. Is it right here? Is it that he's not the one for me? That the person who will choose me and choose us, and love us and appreciate me and who wants to be with me and who thinks we're worth it is still out there? That I haven't found him yet? That the best part of AH is my daughter?

I can't tell if everything that is happening is a sign for me to leave the situation. I want to be strong for Ara. I want to do right by her. Is it time to leave?

But at the same time—maybe when it's time I won't be so questioning. Like, I'll just know.

I'm feeling so vulnerable and so exposed. So...attacked all the time. At this point, I deal with 30 employees and I'm just learning to be a manager. Thank god for Al-Anon, right? Very useful skills....But still. Between him and them? It's too much.

I don't know how to balance not having expectations (premeditated resentments) without losing all hope of a better life. Reality is banging on my door constantly—finding pills, drinking again, being an asshole, resisting positive change, not having a marriage....And I find it nearly impossible to cope. To have hope that things will ever get better.

Because at the end of the day, I do love him. Did love him? Do love him. And I want him to be the person I want him to be. And the person he could be. Which, again, is an expectation. And not embracing Step One [We admit we are powerless over alcohol—that our lives have become unmanageable].

Do you see my dilemma?

I pray and I cry and I beg and I ask for help. I ask for forgiveness because part of me thinks that I deserve this because of how I acted before, with Michael [ex-husband; treating him so badly at the end of our marriage—his name has been changed], *and that I am doomed to this lot in life. On a good day, most of me knows that's not true. But on a bad day? Or week? Or month?*

I'm just tired. And angry. And lonely. So lonely. So angry. So tired of it all.

But I want to be a good mom.

Please. Help. Me.

* * * *

Scott

July 11, 2011

Like we normally did, Shaaren, Ara and I went over to Argo for dinner. But it had been a long drive back from Massachusetts and my nerves were shot. I was already mad - I wouldn't have even had to go up there if Shaaren hadn't run away with our daughter.

Even though I had been attending AA meetings for years, I walked behind the bar like I usually did and poured half a beer. I put the beer down and waited for Shaaren to turn her back, a trick I *thought* I had perfected. But Shaaren turned around as soon as I started chugging. Predictably, she went home with Ara. I was so pissed when the two of them walked out! I was so angry at Shaaren for catching me that I decided to go for broke. I started drinking heavily and taking more and more Adderall - even snorting it. What did I have to lose? I knew my marriage was over anyway.

Most of that night is a blur. I don't remember the details of what I did. The pain and confusion of trying to play both sides had become too much. I was certain this was the end of my family life. My wife could no longer put up with me. I would probably never see my daughter again.

I was mentally and physically exhausted. I was alone and I couldn't stop my brain from tossing hardball questions at me:

What kind of life did I want? Did I want a family and a business—a *real* life? Or did I want to continue with the constant turmoil, the shell of a life I was living, working just to get fucked up, not caring about anyone or anything?

Did I want to be alone, just me, trying to finish off the job I started many years ago: a slow and painful death? Or did I want Shaaren and Ara?

Once more, I was on the verge of losing the people I loved because of my addiction. Here I was, eleven years after killing my mom, and nothing had changed.

I was torn.

CHAPTER 2

Scott

Even though I was incoherent, the situation I was in did cause me to think about my life. How did I end up here?

Who was I kidding? How did I *not* end up here? My life, so far, had pretty much been a road map to this particular moment, the only real questions being:

"How did I make it this far?" and "How was I still alive?"

I was supposed to be born on Christmas Day, 1978. But I guess I got restless and decided to check in a couple weeks early. I showed up in San Diego, California, on December 12 at a whopping two pounds, nine ounces. I've been told that I was so small that my parents had to feed me with a special bottle. Since then, I've stayed on the small side. Everything but my ego, or at least that's what my wife would say.

For the first five and a half years of my life, I stayed put in San Diego where my father, a Navy officer, was stationed. My world was upended for the first time in 1984 when my dad was transferred to Thurso, an ancient town on the north coast of Scotland with a climate similar to Alaska and Iceland. I was forced to trade in sunny, 80-degree days for 50 degrees and rain all the time. I went from being a blond-haired kid with a golden tan to a pasty white one with brown hair and asthma.

In some ways I was lucky in Scotland. Most of the American kids—including my brother Matt, who was four years older than me—had a hard time being accepted by some of the Scottish kids. I'm not sure if it was my good looks, wit, or charm, but I managed to fit right in with the Scots! Who knows, maybe it was just because of my name.

Scott as a young boy

One day, I noticed a bunch of Scottish kids throwing rocks by a stream. "I like to throw rocks," I thought to myself, and headed over to join in. As I got a little closer I noticed that the rocks they were throwing were aimed at my brother. As I ran over to try and help him, I was hit in the head with a rock. I wish I could say it was that rock that made me a raging alcoholic and drug addict not too many years later, but it wasn't. All that rock did was make me bleed.

In 1986 while we were in Scotland, my mother began to have health problems. She was told she needed to be put on the kidney transplant list and had to return to the U.S. to start dialysis. My brother Matt and I headed back to the States with her while my father finished his tour in Scotland. The plan was for my mother to stay with Navy friends from California who were now stationed in the Washington, D.C., area until my father got stateside. But she was in no shape to take care of us at this point. My brother and I were sent to live with my maternal grandparents in Cape Girardo, Missouri. From that point on, I have always referred to Missouri as "Misery". If I thought it was hard going to Scotland, it was even worse coming back to Midwest America. I had returned with a Scottish accent that everyone made fun of, especially since my name was Scott. And, to add insult to injury, I was held back a grade because of the difference in school systems. I hated everything about the place. Could it be that the shock and trauma of such a difficult situation at such a young age was the reason I became an alcoholic and drug addict? I doubt it. Thankfully, my brother and I only had to endure Misery for six months.

In 1987, life returned to normal. My dad had just been stationed at the Pentagon, and my parents bought a home in the Maryland suburb of Germantown. My brother and I settled in and we each began making our own friends. And I started playing baseball. In fact, baseball became a huge part of my life. At the age of ten, I also started my first business and learned to work hard. I would find lost balls on the golf course at the country club near my family's house and sell them back to the golfers. It was a very profitable job for a fifth grader. My only expense was a ball retriever. By the age of thirteen, I was driving my father's lawn mower through the neighborhood cutting grass and washing cars. I discovered I was good at earning money. But I was even better at spending it.

From a very young age I could never sit still. I always had to be on the move, out and about. And I talked and talked. Out of desperation, my parents and even my grandparents would sometimes offer to pay me just to shut up. They'd bet on how long I could keep quiet. If I didn't say a word for half an hour, for example, they'd give me five bucks. It was tough but I managed. I wanted the money. Early on, I earned the nickname "Motor Mouth," and it stuck through middle school, where I was voted "Most Talkative."

After four years in Germantown, we were on the move once again. My father got orders to join the USS John F. Kennedy, an aircraft carrier stationed out of Norfolk, Virginia. I was in sixth grade at the time and my brother had just started high school. There was just enough difference in our ages that we never attended the same school together. But even if we had, our friends were always completely different types. I never had a problem with this. I was quite happy to be left to my own devices.

I didn't have much trouble with the move. Both in Maryland and then in Virginia Beach, I got by in school without putting in much effort and I excelled on the baseball field. I've always been pretty laid back, had been given the gift of self-confidence, and had a knack for being lucky, as well as loyal. I found it easy to strike up a conversation with just about anyone and made new friends wherever I went. Those talents served me well as we moved from place to place. Or maybe, moving from place to place gave me these talents.

At the time, I had no idea how much this constant moving would affect my life and relationships as I grew older. Through all the moves my family made, I simply adjusted—fitting in on a beach in California or Virginia, in a different country, in the Midwest, or anywhere else. Now I realize that because of all this moving around and fitting in, I never really figured out who *I* was or what *I* stood for. I had a mask for every place, time and situation. This was both a blessing and a curse. It certainly helped me later in my professional life—bartenders need to be able to chat up anybody. But I had no clue who I really was as a person.

My dad was gone a good deal of the time when I was growing up, either out to sea or working late. When we were in Virginia Beach, my dad's ship, the USS Kennedy, saw action during the first Gulf War and he was away for six to nine months. When he was home, he tried to discipline me but I didn't listen. Even if I did pay attention, I always seemed to find a way to manipulate the situation in order to get out of trouble. If I did get grounded, I'd go up to my room and clean it up or straighten out my closet. Then I'd go to my mom and all was forgiven.

As my teenage years set in, I was growing more and more uncomfortable with myself. On the outside I was confident and outgoing, but on the inside I felt lonely and scared. Was this normal? Did everyone feel this way? I didn't let anyone get close to me for fear of being hurt. During all my moving around, I had mastered the art of seeming close but keeping my distance. I learned to do whatever was needed to fit in. I didn't reveal myself, if I even knew what that self was. Added to my unspoken fears was the fact that my mind was racing about 500 miles an hour all the time and I couldn't turn it off. (My ADHD wouldn't be diagnosed until much later.) But, at the time, I didn't know what my problem was.

At the end of the summer before my freshman year of high school, my parents left for a few days to take my brother to college at Georgia Southern University in Statesboro, Georgia. Like many kids my age who have the house to themselves, I threw a party. The guest of honor was Mary Jane. From the first time I smoked, I *loved* Mary Jane. Everything finally slowed down in my head and life became fun. From the age of fourteen until well into my mid-twenties, pot was an everyday thing. Wake-n-bake and then smoke all day.

Throughout high school I was a stoner *and* an athlete. Looking back, I can see how much my life was shaped on the ball fields of Little Creek Naval Base. And how intertwined drugs and baseball were. My first cigarette, my first joint, my first drink, line, mushroom, pill, hit. They all happened at the field or somewhere else with my baseball friends.

When I was fourteen, I got my first restaurant job—washing dishes at a place called Anchor Inn. A lot of my philosophy for life took shape at that job: Work Hard, Party Harder! It would be my motto for a long time. My drinking started to take off as well. Pot had become my everyday crutch by this time. But I needed something else to blow off steam. I found alcohol.

My friends were the cooks, servers and bartenders at the restaurant and I felt I had to be able to keep up with them. We would steal cases of beer from the walk-in fridge and hide them in the dumpster area for when we got off work. From the start of high school and beyond—with the exception of my baseball team—almost all my friends were much older. I had very few friends my own age and high school became an afterthought. I could do the bare minimum and still pass my courses with average grades.

From the beginning, my drinking was anything but normal. I had my first real bender when I was fifteen and I went to visit my brother at his college. The first thing he said to me when I arrived was: "Don't get all fucked up on the first night." Of course, I got wasted! So wasted that I blacked out and woke up in a recliner. It was not a pretty picture. I had thrown up on myself and crapped my pants. Still pretty drunk and feeling worse than I ever had, I figured out which of my brother's friends smoked pot and went to hang out with them. Busy as I was hanging out and smoking pot, I still found time to purchase my first pitcher of beer at a bar. I threw up a lot during that visit but I continued to drink every night I was there. By the time I got home I had sworn off alcohol. In fact, just the smell of liquor made me sick for a long time. Until it didn't.

In December 1994, I found myself in the middle of an LSD deal. I knew someone who had it and I knew someone who wanted it and I figured I could earn a little money making everyone happy. We were standing in the middle of the hallway on the second floor of the school, hanging out like we always did. The seller, another student who was probably two years ahead of me, was giving me the hits (each one wrapped in aluminum foil). Then a teacher walked around the corner and caught us.

I was expelled from high school.

I was promptly shipped off to a private boarding school called the Miller School of Albemarle in Charlottesville, Virginia. As many schools had done after World War II, it had developed a military program and we had to wear uniforms—every day! The only uniform I was used to was my father's, and the only one I had ever worn was when I played baseball. I had the second half of that school year to focus almost completely on schoolwork, although I did play on the tennis team and was a member of the ski club. During that time, I earned a 3.5 GPA, made the Dean's List, and was well-liked by everyone. The school offered me a full scholarship to come back the following year. I turned it down mainly because there was no baseball program and I missed my friends. I was probably also thinking it was time to get back to my old habits.

That fall I returned to Frank W. Cox High School, which had expelled me as a freshman nine months earlier. I figured they were willing to take me back because I hadn't been in any trouble since then, my grades at the Miller School were good, and I had obviously "learned my lesson." Sure. During my sophomore year at Cox, my GPA slipped to 2.0, but who cared? I had baseball and pot back in my life. Despite the pot, I was a varsity starter from that year on (one of only two sophomores chosen that year). In my junior year, 1995-1996, our ball team—the Falcons—won the Virginia AAA State Championship and was ranked one of the Top 20 Teams in the country by *USA Today*.

My attitude toward school changed after that win. My GPA was on the rise and I was starting to think about playing college baseball somewhere after graduation. As senior year began, my GPA was close to 3.0. But with a D in Government, I had no chance of making the honor roll.

"If you can't get a report card without a D on it," my father said, "I'm not going to pay for college."

I was devastated. And pissed!

It's hard to admit, but I can see now that my father was right. I had no business going to college. Simply put, it would have been a bad investment. *I was a bad investment.* I have to give my dad a lot of credit. He came from a large family in the Midwest. I think he used the Navy to get away from there, see the world, and make a good life for himself, my mother and his kids. I realize now that my father was much smarter than I gave him credit for at the time.

Probably the smartest investment he made was taking out a life insurance policy on me when I was a teenager. Maybe, like many people (including myself), he thought I would live a short life. I didn't find out about the policy until later, when I got married—when I was meeting with a financial planner. At first, the way he made it sound, I thought he had gotten it when I was really young, but it turns out that my father had taken it out after I was well onto my self-destructive path.

Because my road to college had turned into a dead end, I dropped most of my classes for the spring semester of my senior year and took only the bare minimum needed to graduate. I was in a Marketing Program at school that let you out early if you had a job to go to. A friend's father, who owned a construction company, had hired me to run errands. By this time, my father and I weren't getting along at all. In fact, I hated him, I hated the military, and I hated the fact that he was trying to push me to join the military.

By contrast, my mother and I were always really close. Even though she worked most of the time I was growing up, she was the one who really ran the house. And she came to *all* my baseball games. My father, not so much. Of course, he had to be away a lot of the time. That was his job. If I ever needed anything, I always went to my mother. She spoiled me. She was my rock. I knew she would always be there for me. I think my mom understood how hard it was to grow up in a military household, constantly moving from place to place. If my father understood, he never talked about it.

My mother had been sick a lot during my childhood because of her kidney disease. She had her first kidney transplant in 1987, when I was nine. During my senior year of high school, my mother got sick again.

Her kidney was failing and she needed another transplant. I volunteered one of mine. I went through all the donor tests and found out I matched up very well. In fact, there was a 99% chance that a donated kidney from me would last my mother for the rest of her life. I was all ready to do it, but my mother decided at the last minute that she couldn't go through with it. She felt it was more important for me to play baseball and finish my senior year of high school.

She was put on the national kidney transplant list once again. I think we all felt that she wouldn't have a problem finding a kidney through the transplant list. In the meantime, she could continue to do dialysis at home until a kidney was located for her. Once she had made her decision, I put it out of my mind and went on with my life, such as it was.

CHAPTER 3

Scott

After barely graduating high school in 1997, I started working for a Virginia Beach heating and air conditioning company that a friend's father owned. My parents had told me they would be moving to Annandale in Northern Virginia at the end of the year because my father, now a lieutenant commander, was retiring from the Navy. I needed to start thinking about what I wanted to do. A few weeks later, my parents said their plans had changed. They would be moving over the summer—in about a month. Now I really had to find somewhere to live soon or I'd be moving with them.

I found an apartment a few blocks from the beach at the corner of 17th and Biltmore Streets, close to the tourist area. It was a one bedroom in what looked like an old motel that had been turned into rental units. There was even a swimming pool. It was a decent apartment for someone right out of high school and, at $435 a month, it was a good deal. I got a night job cooking at Hammerheads, a bar on the Virginia Beach tourist strip that would help supplement my income. That was the plan, anyway.

I was eighteen years old, living on my own, working the heating/ac job during the day and cooking at Hammerheads at night. I would close up the kitchen at 10:00 p.m. each night and start drinking at the bar, hanging out with the bartenders and cocktail servers. My serious blackouts started around this time. I would stay out drinking until 2:00 a.m., head back to my apartment and crash for a few hours, then get up at 6:00 a.m. for my day job. I still remember working in airless attics in the middle of summer after a night of drinking. It was awful. I spent much of my time lying in peoples' front yards because I was about to pass out from the heat.

By this time, working at the bar had taken priority over my day job. I started using cocaine on a regular basis so I could drink even longer. This drug-alcohol combination would be my standard operating procedure for the next few years.

By my nineteenth birthday in December 1997, I should have had two DUIs. I don't even remember what I was doing that got me the first one. I do remember that for some reason my case was continued for six months. When I finally went to court, I learned that the case had been thrown out because the police officer who charged me had been terminated from the force.

For what should have been my second DUI, I managed to flip my Jeep over in a residential area shortly after leaving one of the beach bars with a bunch of friends. We all got out of the Jeep safely and no one was hurt, but right away we heard shouting from nearby houses. I switched fleeces with my friend, Keith, because I was worried I could be identified by what I was wearing. That was my brilliant drunk logic. Of course, we never put it together that the people in the houses probably saw what *all of us* had on.

One of my friends grabbed my cell phone and reported that my Jeep had been stolen while we were at a local bar. Then we all took off toward the beach. I figured a run along the beach would be the quickest way back to the bar. By the time I got there, the black pants I was wearing were covered with sand because I was so drunk I kept falling down. The police were already at the bar and an officer called my parents. When they arrived, the police told us they had found my Jeep and asked if we wanted to go see it. Of course I said yes. I was still pretending it had been stolen!

Eventually, I admitted that it was my vehicle and I had been in it when it flipped over. The police couldn't prove I had been driving, so I was identified as a "passenger at the scene." They gave me a number of tickets, including "leaving the scene of an accident," "reckless driving," and "filing a false police report." My blood alcohol level tested over three times the legal limit (which was .10 back then). Fortunately, I had a very good Virginia Beach lawyer, whom my parents paid for. I escaped with only a misdemeanor charge. I can see now that getting off so easy was maybe not the best thing that could have happened to me.

I felt invincible.

By the time I reached my twentieth birthday, my parents were basically paying my rent. Even though I was working two jobs, I could barely survive because of my drinking and drug habits. I would talk to my mom on the phone and tell her I didn't have enough money to cover my rent. Then she'd make a deposit in my account. I felt bad about doing this, but not bad enough to change my behavior and be more responsible. And there really was no incentive to change. I kept getting pulled out of all the messes I created.

Employees working at Hammerheads got good discounts on both food and drinks. For example, we were only charged a dollar for a beer, and we didn't even have to pay for it in cash. The bartenders kept our tab and management would just deduct the money from our next paycheck. One week, during which I had worked twenty-five hours, my paycheck was sixty-five cents.

Do the math. I was working to pay for my drinking.

For the longest time, I actually used to wonder why the cops always seemed to target me while I was driving. I mean, I was pulled over *a lot*. I'm still not sure if it was my constant speeding or my license plate, which read IRIE VIB. Irie [eye-ree] Vibe—for anyone who doesn't know—is the happy feeling you get when you're high. Or maybe the cops didn't care for the huge sticker of an alien with dreads and a rasta hat on my back window. Or maybe all the Bob Marley stickers. *What was their problem?* I was a pothead and proud of it, and yet I still couldn't see what trouble that was causing me!

My life was obviously out of control. Even I knew that. My parents were concerned about me and my mother's health was getting much worse. She convinced me to come to Northern Virginia and live with them for a while. I decided it would be a good move. I knew I needed to get out of Virginia Beach because my luck was running out.

At the hearing for my last trip to court in Virginia Beach for the "leaving the scene" charges in the flipped Jeep incident, the judge went through both city and state ordinances *trying very hard* to find a way to throw me in jail. Since I was one of the first cases called that day, I felt bad for everyone else waiting in the courtroom.

The judge finally gave up in disgust and she gave me the max the guidelines called for, which was just a $250 fine with no jail time. As I was heading toward the courtroom door, I heard the judge's voice.

"Mr. Magnuson!" she called out.

"Yes, Judge?" I said, turning to face her.

"If I ever catch you in my courtroom again you *will* go to jail!"

Yes, it was definitely a good time to leave Virginia Beach.

CHAPTER 4

Scott

In 1998, I moved back in with my parents. I was 20.

I hated Northern Virginia. I hardly knew anyone there and the area was so different from what I was used to. I missed the laid back vibe of the beach. I had no clue how to meet anyone on this new terrain. And besides, when I did go out, I always used my fake ID because I was still under the legal drinking age. So who was I supposed to be anyway? I found the whole place so buttoned down and uptight. The first question people would always ask me was "What do you do for a living?" This was followed quickly by "What kind of car do you drive?" I was twenty years old. I was living with my parents. I wasn't going to college. It was humiliating. I had no plan, no idea what I wanted to do with my "life". All the stupid questions people asked just reminded me of how unhappy I was with my current situation. Of course, *I* was never the one at fault. I never took responsibility for my own actions—or inaction. I did hear one thing loud and clear, though. It was definitely time to get a new car.

And a new car didn't seem that far off, because at least I was making some money. I had been lucky enough to find a job running the production department for K & E Printing and Graphics in Merrifield, a suburb of Fairfax County, not too long a drive via the Capital Beltway from my parents' house in Annandale. When I moved in with my parents, I was still driving the Jeep Cherokee I had flipped and reported stolen in Virginia Beach. The passenger side that it slid on was a mess. Driving around

Northern Virginia where all anyone seemed to care about was the car you drove was getting to me. By age twenty, I had already managed to destroy or otherwise disable three cars. The first was a Plymouth Horizon. After I put that out of commission, I got a Honda Accord. I eventually sold that to a friend so I could buy the Jeep. This time I really wanted a sports car! I bought a Mitsubishi Eclipse GS-T. It was Everett Green with a metallic clear coat.

One night, I was at a friend's house just sitting around watching a Mike Tyson fight on TV and getting a decent buzz on. After a while I got bored and decided to head out and find a bar. All the beer I had been drinking was making me sleepy. I thought I needed some liquor and a little livelier atmosphere. Driving down Route 1 in Arlington, I spotted the Crystal City Sports Pub on 23ʳᵈ Street. I parked my new little sports car across the street and headed for the bar where I sat drinking for a few hours. Around 12:30 a.m., I decided to call it a night. I walked outside and made it halfway across the street before I noticed four cops standing around and talking near my car. A police cruiser was parked just behind my car.

For some reason, I decided it would be smarter to continue what now looked like a *very* long trek across the street to the Eclipse, get in, and simply drive away. I was really wasted and I'm sure I must have stumbled the rest of the way to my car. I didn't say anything to the cops, just got in and drove off. The cops must have had a good laugh about me being so obviously drunk and then driving away right in front of them. As soon as I turned the corner, a police car pulled me over. As the cop got out and walked over to the driver's side window, I stuffed my fake ID and stash of pot under my seat.

The first thing out of the cop's mouth was, "How much money you got on you?" I told him about 100 bucks. He opened my car door, motioned me to get out, and offered me a seat on the curb. I sat there and watched as he searched the Eclipse. He looked under the seat. Then he looked back at me and smiled.

"Here's what we're going to do," he said as he took the $100 from my wallet. "I am going to have your car towed to the impound lot. You can pick it up tomorrow. And you are going to call a cab."

"How am I going to pay for it?" I asked.

"That's not my problem," he said.

When the cop drove off, I started walking down Route 1, cussing and kicking the ground. The more I walked, the more pissed I got. That asshole took all my money! I finally called a friend and persuaded him to come pick me up. Of course, when my friend arrived, he saw right away how totally fucked up I was. I almost got in a fight with him as he tried to convince me that I was lucky. But I wasn't going to listen to anyone.

The next day I went to the impound lot to retrieve my car. I was told I needed the correct paperwork from the courthouse to get the car released. When I got to the courthouse, they told me my car had been towed as a "citizen's request" and I didn't need any paperwork. Back I went to the impound lot. When I finally got in my car I was relieved to find my fake ID and stash still under the seat right where I had "hid" them the night before. I guess that cop did me a couple of favors that night.

Alcohol was not the only thing I was using to dull the pain and boredom of Northern Virginia and my life. I found myself in the drug world full time. I had touched base again with my friend Johnny [name has been changed]. He was a year or two older than I was, but we had lived in the same neighborhood in Virginia Beach and graduated from the same high school. Even though he had moved to Northern Virginia, we had stayed in touch while I was still in Virginia Beach. He had even come down to Virginia Beach to help me move. Now we started hanging out together a lot and I helped him with his "delivery" business, both the legal and not-so-legal side of it. We stayed up all night doing cocaine—snorting it, smoking it, we didn't care how. On weekends, we would take off to visit friends who were in college, drinking and doing coke the whole trip there. And we would go to raves. I once did twelve pills of Ecstasy in two days, followed by a bottle of K (Special K or Ketamine).

By 1999 my mother was really sick. She had been on the donor list for the past three years, but no compatible kidney had become available. She asked me to go through the tests again to see if I could still give her one of my kidneys. Of course I said yes. Both my parents knew I had drug and alcohol problems, but they had no idea of the extent of my addiction. I went through tests at Inova Fairfax Hospital and was told I couldn't donate because of my drug use. My mother didn't ask and I couldn't bear to tell her why I couldn't give her a kidney. Nobody talked to me about getting clean—maybe she needed my kidney faster than I could have gone through that process? And who was I kidding? I didn't want to get clean, anyway.

In late November, my mother got a call from the doctor at Sentara Norfolk General Hospital who had treated her when we lived in Virginia Beach. He said they might have a kidney for her. Of course, they would have to do stress tests first to make sure her heart was strong enough to handle the kidney transplant surgery. I was so happy, both for her and for myself! Now I'd never have to tell my parents why I couldn't give my mother a kidney. My dad drove my mom down to Norfolk around December 1.

Since I was still working full time, I stayed in Annandale and waited for news. I was expecting someone to call any time and tell me her transplant surgery was a success. Instead, when the call came, I was told that my mother had suffered a serious heart attack during a stress test and was in the Intensive Care Unit. I needed to get down to Norfolk right away.

I couldn't believe this was happening.

My brother Matt drove up from Atlanta, where he was now living, and met me and my father at the hospital. I spent most of December 1999 there. My mother was mostly unconscious when I sat by her bed in the ICU. Once in a while she would wake up, but she couldn't speak. She just smiled and gave me that loving look with her big eyes.

The hospital staff was kind enough to set aside a room for our family to use while my mom was in the ICU. I tried to stay close by, pacing the hospital halls to pass the time. Now and then I would take the elevator down to the ground floor and go outside for a smoke.

But just waiting around with nothing to do was making me stir crazy. I finally decided to take a night off. I needed to let loose, see some old friends, and "clear my head." Of course, I went straight to Hammerheads. Waking up in jail the next morning was not part of my plan. I certainly had no clue how I got there. From what I was told, police officers had found me crawling through someone's bushes with no shirt on, in a state of mild hypothermia. I had lost my cell phone, which was probably a good thing, considering all the desperate calls I must have missed. Once I sobered up, the police released me. I lucked out. Johnny was visiting his parents, who still lived in Virginia Beach. He picked me up and drove me back to the hospital.

I walked in with a pocket full of court summonses, including "drunk in public," "possession of marijuana," and "trespassing." I must have been quite a sight and probably smelled worse than the hospital bedpans. My father pressed me on where I had been. I threw the court papers at him and said, "What do you want me to tell you? I've been in fucking jail!"

On my twenty-first birthday, December 12, 1999, my mother's doctors told me she was going to die. My mom was now on life support, she was sedated, and the doctors were just trying to keep her as comfortable as possible. It was the end. For two weeks between my birthday and Christmas, I watched my mother slip in and out of consciousness as her friends came to say goodbye. My father had made the decision to have her taken off life support after our family and friends had a chance to see her.

On Christmas day, my brother and I said goodbye to our mother for the last time. The Wilkinses (parents of my friend Byron) invited me over to their house for Christmas. It was one of the nicest things anyone could have done. They even went out and bought me a few presents. I will never forget it. I left the next day to head back to Northern Virginia and Matt returned to Georgia. We had already said goodbye to our mother, and my father didn't think Matt and I should wait around for her to die.

The doctors expected my mother to die very soon after she was taken off life support. But my mom managed to hold on for a week and make it to the turn of the century. My mother, Donna Magnuson, died on New Year's Day 2000. She was fifty years old.

My mother's body was cremated at a local funeral home and my dad decided it made sense to have her funeral service in Virginia Beach as well—at Bayside Presbyterian Church. It was the church our family had attended for many years and it was right around the corner from the house where I grew up. On January 3, 2000, I drove back down to Virginia Beach. The service was held a day or two later. It was nice. A bagpiper played and all of my friends from the area came, as well as many of my family's friends. A reception was held after the service at our old next door neighbor's house. Of course, my friends and I got high on our way over.

After the funeral, I headed back to Northern Virginia. My mother's ashes went to Cape Girardeau, Missouri, and now rest in the same cemetery where her parents are buried.

I will always remember my mother's smile. She was the heart and rock of our family and the best mom anyone could hope for. I think now that if I could just manage to become half the person she was, I would be satisfied. But at the time, all I felt was a crushing emptiness and guilt. I knew I was to blame for her death.

My mother's doctors in Norfolk had assured me that even if we could have gone through with the kidney transplant surgery using one of my kidneys, my mother would have died of heart failure on the operating table. And I would have lost a kidney for no reason.

I didn't believe them.

I was sure I could have saved my mom's life pretty much any time since high school, but my addiction took priority.

How could I love drinking and drugs more than my own mother?

I am still haunted by this: My mother's life was in my hands and I let her die.

CHAPTER 5

Shaaren

I couldn't believe that I was here again.

With one failed marriage already, and another failing (could I really blame Scott's addiction?), at some point I'd have to concede that the common factor was me. Being surprised was laughable, really. How would any relationship that began as an affair ever last?

Didn't I know from the beginning he had problems? Did I really think I could change him? Wasn't I broken myself when our relationship started? Hadn't I maybe even been a little bit broken my whole life?

In the beginning, we made so much sense together (to us, anyway), but looking back through years of denial, heartache, and trauma, it was hard to imagine how this current situation wouldn't have been the outcome.

I am the oldest child of former, self-described hippies. Along with a younger brother and sister, I grew up in the small town of Groton, Massachusetts, where I lived with my family until I left for college. I imagine my parents picked Groton, which is about twenty-five miles north and west of Boston (close to the New Hampshire border), because it had good schools and they found a house they liked on a lot of land. It was a quintessential, New England, white clapboard house with a wrap-around porch (and rocking chairs, of course) on a tree-lined street. As far back as I can remember, my parents always kept a garden, canned a lot of food, and made their own maple syrup.

Life moved slowly, too. It was probably my perception as a kid more than Groton itself, but back then, the weeks in between things (December 'til Christmas—what we celebrated, the last month of school before vacation, the beginning of summer break 'til the start of school) all lasted forever. I guess that's kind of what being a kid is like—not knowing that eventually time speeds up, life moves faster, and some of the things that were so magical lose their luster. But somehow, in a small town, when you're little, and where almost everybody is on the same calendar, time feels larger than life.

Shaaren as a young girl

I've had some of the same friends since I was a small child. This continuity in relationships has probably made me overly trusting of *new* friends—sometimes to my own regret. I often think that every new friend will be one for life—an assumption that's clearly not very realistic or fair. Even through some of the disappointment, though, I'm not convinced this isn't the better way to be. Being optimistic versus jaded, where everyone is full of possibility and not weighed down by my skepticism?

The town has grown a lot since I was a kid there, but I can still remember when we got our first stop light (blinking yellow) as well as 911 direct calling. Before that, you had to dial an actual phone number to get the combined police station, town hall, fire department, and superintendent's office. I also remember when we were no longer able to simply dial the last four digits of a phone number to reach another house in town. To this day I'm more of a "turn left at the big red barn and if you get to a statue you've gone too far" kind of direction-giver as opposed to knowing street names and route numbers. As a result, I have a terrible sense of direction. Thank goodness for GPS!

New England falls meant playing in leaf piles when we were kids and raking leaf piles when we were teenagers. Making apple pies for the annual church sale, adjusting to life back in school, and soccer. Winters were for building snow forts, sipping hot chocolate and hope, hope, hoping for snow days. Springs were muddy and late, but always a welcome sight after a long winter. And of course, more soccer. And summers! Summers were swimming at one of Groton's lake's or ponds, or at one of the pools where one could become a member. Lots of biking and walking around, camps, cicadas and lightening bugs, and fresh basil pesto from the garden.

And always, a couple weeks in Maine where our extended family had a house on the coast.

And then, back to fall. School supplies and new clothes. The humidity lessened, gradually, sound travelled further, and one could once again hear mourning doves cooing in the distance.

I know it's tempting to idealize small towns, and there is a lot that is wonderful about them. But they can be hard - especially for people who are different. As an international and transracial adoptee, it was very difficult, too.

CHAPTER 6

Shaaren

I was about four months old when I arrived in the United States from India on December 7, 1975. I don't have any birth records naming my first parents or the circumstances of my birth (other than the amended ones that most adoptees have listing adoptive parents as parents), but the general assumption seems to be that I was born sometime in August 1975. Despite always being celebrated on August 10th, I have since found out that my adoptive parents picked that "birthday" themselves.

It's a horrible thing to not really know when you were born.

Or where.

Or to whom.

My adoptive mother had grown up across the street from a childhood friend who later arranged adoptions from India with Mother Teresa. I was placed through one of Mother Teresa's Missionaries of Charity (New Delhi orphanage).

I have absolutely no information about my origins other than my birth country, and I'm not sure anybody else has information about me, either. If they do, they're certainly not sharing it. I've since spoken with the woman who arranged my adoption and written to the hospital closest to my orphanage, but have found no information. This devastating lack of access to information about our origins is common for domestic as well as international adoptees in closed adoptions (especially from 40 years ago) and it is painful in a way that only adoptees (and first families?) can understand.

Several years after I came to live with them, my brother, Raji, who is fourteen months younger than I am, and also from India, joined us as well. My sister, Marissa, who is five years younger than me, is my parents' biological child. Given that my adoptive parents are white and my brother and I are people of color, there was never any "big reveal" or hidden secret that we were both adoptees.

Growing up, I had things in common with my family, but I still didn't feel related to them in the same way that most non-adoptees are connected to family. While genes aren't everything, they are powerful. In large family gatherings, being surrounded by people who look and act similarly to each other was difficult; a reminder of how much I longed to have that in my life. I really have no way of telling where I got what: who I look like, where I got my laugh, or who else has my crooked fingers. I may be almost forty years old, but not knowing who I am feels as raw now as it did when I was a kid.

Imagine for a moment being the only person in the world you know you're related to.

Being an adoptee is a journey, and each adoptee is on a different part of that journey. At times, it can be a very painful one, and other times, we're able to put it on the back burner, so to speak. For some of us, it's easier to deny that anything bothers us and just block out any "adoption stuff" rather than admit how isolating it can be.

"Adoption loss is the only trauma in the world where the victims are expected by the whole of society to be grateful." (Reverend Keith C Griffith, MBE) If my entire family had died in a car accident, I would be afforded the time and space to grieve such a loss. With adoption, which is also losing an entire family, adoptees aren't given that same space. And even worse, society expects us to not only forget, but be thankful for this loss. Such gratefulness can be especially difficult for us transracial adoptees, who have often grown up with the additional hardship of overt racism and prejudice in our own families and/or our own communities.

Navigating a small, white town was challenging, and I had my share of painful times. In elementary school, I was called names like "brownie."

And even though most kids outgrew the terminology, many didn't lose the sentiment. When I was in eighth grade, a classmate told me I would only be "dateable" if I had "a race change." I also remember the phrase "go back where [you/he/she/they] came from" being thrown around a bit. Even teachers, "Shaaren! *You* know about the tsetse fly, right?" "What? No." "Yes! The tsetse fly! From *Africa*!"

Often, when I left our house, people would yell things at me from passing cars. Plus the staring, wherever I went. And the constant, intrusive, "othering" questions: "Where are you from?" "Massachusetts." "No, where are you from *really?*" "Massachusetts." "No. Like, where is your *family* from?" "Massachusetts." "I mean your relatives. *Originally.*" Or comments "You're really well-spoken". "Wow. You're so articulate." Add to that a complete lack of seeing myself positively reflected in my community and my family—or even reflected at all—and you can imagine the toll it took.

Although I didn't have the vocabulary for it then, dealing with these *constant* and cumulative racial aggressions and micro-aggressions, coupled with being raised without the skills or support to handle them (or flat out being told my opinions were wrong "Oh, Shaaren. That's not racist.") made me *extremely* angry. And with no counter-narrative to help embrace -or even acknowledge- a positive racial identity made me *really* sad.

What I really needed was for somebody to acknowledge how hard it was living like this. Unrelated to anybody, alone in the world, with a white family who couldn't and didn't understand what it was like. Instead, I was forced into therapy because I was so angry, as if I had nothing to be angry about.

To cope, I started cutting myself. I didn't do it all the time, but for years it offered me an enormous amount of relief from all these intense feelings. And somehow it helped me bridge my two personalities—the outward one where everything was fine, and the internal one where I was hanging on by a thread.

It's often said that we adoptees know what we stand for, but not necessarily who we are. I think growing up this way forced me to figure out what I stood for early on, and really helped me decide on the paths I would take later in my life. I saw myself as a voice for all underdogs, all things liberal, and all children. And I'm not sure I've changed much in that regard.

I'd also probably attribute some of my choices along the way to being abandoned and failed by all the adults who were supposed to care or advocate for me.

Whatever the underlying reasons, my values determined everything—my choices in friends, where I went to college, my career, my personal decisions later on, and my absolute love of (and extreme patience for) children.

Despite not fitting in all the time in these white spaces, I made some of the best friends. I'm not sure what I would have done without them. And even though it was hard, I think that I was a fairly well-adjusted kid who took the prospect of a bright future and went after it.

CHAPTER 7

Shaaren

I have always loved and been great with kids. I started babysitting at age eleven, when, for all intents and purposes, I was still a kid myself. Outside of school, sports, and friends, that's what I did—took care of other peoples' kids. I was also very frugal, even miserly. Once the money I earned went into my bank account, it never came out. I think my first withdrawal might have been when I went off to college!

When I was fourteen, I shaved my head. I had one of those haircuts that many guys had in the late 1980s and early '90s. It was kind of a bowl cut, but long on top and shaved underneath. Eventually, I got tired of it, but I didn't want to bother taking the time to grow it out so I decided just to shave it off. My best friend Christy and I went to a hair salon in our town and off it came (leaving some bangs in front). And it stayed off for the next eight years. Eventually, I did the shaving myself, since it had to be done every week.

I never smoked in high school, never did drugs, and I didn't really drink until I went to college. I didn't listen to that much Top-40 music either. I preferred the Violent Femmes, The Cure, Sinead O'Connor, and They Might Be Giants. This may not sound terribly counterculture now, but those groups weren't really popular in my town at the time. I also listened to some of my parents' music from the 1960s like Simon and Garfunkel and Joan Baez. And Christy and I loved to listen to WXLO, the oldies station, which played a lot of 1950s and some 1960s songs. Our favorite soundtracks were also pretty far off the beaten path for kids our age: "Beaches," "My Girl," "Toys," and "Thelma & Louise."

Christy and I liked going to the mall (boys!) and I also enjoyed going to Harvard Square (probably because it was trendy and cool and Groton... wasn't). We'd drive to the nearest T station and take the train in—a good hour and a half trip. And I'd daydream about living there (or any city) one day. Along with my Doc Martens, I bought most of my clothes at a store in Harvard Square. I wore a lot of Indian-print wraparound skirts, which were definitely not popular in my school at the time, but I liked them and the price was right. I also played varsity soccer and ran track. I had a core group of good friends and, for the most part, I enjoyed my schoolwork.

Certainly one of the most important influences on me as I was growing up was the Unitarian Universalist Church in Groton. My parents were Unitarian and when we were little, we all attended church together on Sundays. The kids went to part of the church service, then attended the Sunday school—in the winter, anyway. Our church didn't really operate in the summer. Unitarianism has ten basic principles, but there were two that really resonated with me, even early on: "the inherent worth and dignity of every person" and "justice, equity and compassion in human relations." After all these years, I still carry in my wallet the same "What do Unitarian Universalists believe" card I had when I was a teenager.

I also have a wonderful tattoo in the middle of my upper back that I got in my twenties. It's a Unitarian chalice next to a crescent moon with a sun around the edge. I'm not active in the Unitarian Church anymore, although I might be if I wasn't always working on weekends. If you visited my house, however, you'd find seven framed printouts "What do UUs believe?" printed and hanging in the entrance hallway, right above six of Scott's Buddhist quotes.

I was very active in our church. I attended their youth conferences and participated in YRUU (Young Religious Unitarian Universalist) meetings and activities all during my high school years. YRUU is for Unitarians ages fourteen to twenty and encourages youth empowerment, social activism, and leadership. Even though I was known to buy mainstream teen magazines, I looked forward to the YRUU newspaper, *Synapse,* the most. The spring of senior year, my friend Mandy and I drove all night with a Unitarian group to take part in the 1993 March on Washington for "Lesbian, Gay & Bi Equal Rights and Liberation".

Even when I was in college, my minister, Dorothy, asked me to be part of a panel on Grassroots Organizing at a PURPOSE conference (People United for Responsible Policies on Sexuality Education) outside of Boston.

Along with sports and babysitting, I also did a lot of volunteering. As a teenager, I identified with many injustices in the world. I walked or marched or raised money for so many causes that my "superlative" designation in the senior yearbook was "Class Activist." It was a new title created just for me and my friend Jon. I think the class activist designation continued for a few years after I graduated.

Throughout high school, my list of volunteer activities kept growing. I was on the AIDS Action Committee in my town. I lobbied to get condom availability in my high school (denied) and went to Amnesty International meetings. I was also a high school Peer Leader. And the other marches and vigils and walks! For abortion and gay rights, to help the homeless and end hunger, to raise money for food banks, and to stop domestic violence.

Although I was well-liked by my high school classmates, I wouldn't ever say I was "popular." The first party I went to—and it wasn't like I was invited to parties and turned them down—was the big graduation bash at the end of senior year that *everyone* was invited to. As a kind of unofficial designated driver, I drove a couple of people home during the party who didn't have cars or who couldn't drive theirs.

I applied to four liberal arts colleges: Bard College, located along the Hudson River north of New York City; Hampshire College in Amherst, Massachusetts; Eugene Lang College, part of the New School for Social Research (now called the New School for Liberal Arts) in New York City; and Earlham College, a Quaker school in Richmond, Indiana. I received acceptance letters from all four, but Bard and Hampshire seemed a little too close to home, and I don't think they offered me as much scholarship money as the other two. So, in the end, it came down to Earlham and Eugene Lang. Lang had no health care center for students and only offered housing for first year students. Earlham had housing for all four years as well as a better financial aid package. I chose Earlham and have never regretted it.

All my volunteering and activism in high school also earned me a Bonner Scholarship from Earlham and the Bertram and Corella Bonner Foundation as part of my college financial aid package. Unlike work-study, where students work on campus and get paid directly, "Bonners," as we were called, volunteered in the community ten hours each week. The scholarship money went directly to pay our tuition. We were also required to volunteer 280 hours during the summer.

I loved Earlham, the friends I made there, and especially the education I got. Being a Quaker institution, every decision was made through consensus. The process takes a lot longer, but in the end, everybody has been heard and, in theory at least, everybody is at peace with a decision. Quakers also refer to each other on a first-name basis, so I never had a class with "Professor So-and-So". Instead, I was taught by Dan, Steve, Joann, Nelson, Howard, and a number of other extremely talented scholars. I wish everybody could have this kind of education. We were taught to think, to collaborate, to view things globally and act locally. Classes were small— sometimes only seven students; there weren't any multiple choice exams; and nobody was fighting for quarters of a point. Although I know I didn't work up to my full potential, I learned so much. I consider my four years at Earlham a truly invaluable experience.

While I was at Earlham, I participated in a six-month, study abroad program in Bogotá, Colombia. CEUCA (Centro de Estudios Unidos Colombo-Americano), the center where we took classes, also found us host families and helped us adjust. The program no longer exists, but it was wonderful. While I was in Bogotá, I also volunteered at La Liga (La Liga Colombiana de Lucha Contra el SIDA), an HIV education and health project run by and for gay men. I worked on inputting responses from their latest behavior and health survey into the computer.

I graduated from Earlham in 1997 with a B.A. in Human Development and Social Relations (a major that was kind of in between Psych and Sociology and aimed at social service work). I also had a minor in Spanish and a focus in Education. I was good to go.

CHAPTER 8

Scott

The year 2000 was a rough one for me. I can see now that I must have been grieving for my mom and for myself. I was probably also trying to push away the guilt I felt about letting her down in so many ways. But at the time, I don't think I ever really admitted—or even understood—what was going on.

My alcohol and drug use accelerated at a record pace after my mother's death. I was suicidal. I drank, I drove, I hung out with people who were bad for me, and I'm sure I was a bad influence on many others. I just didn't care anymore.

Like many addicts, everything I did had to be done to the extreme. One of the extremes I loved was to drive fast. And my recently acquired Mitsubishi was up to the challenge. I would try to race everything I saw. I used to see how fast I could get from Northern Virginia down to Virginia Beach to visit my old friends. The trip was normally a three- to three-and-a-half-hour drive. My best time? Two hours and fifteen minutes, racing a Mustang Cobra the whole way. Once again, I was invincible. No one could catch me. And I never worried about the police or anyone else getting in my way.

I only had the Mitsubishi for about a year, but in that one year I received six reckless driving tickets for speeding. The worst was getting pulled over on my way back from Virginia Beach at around midnight. Heading west on Route 64 toward Richmond, I was doing 112 miles an hour with my foot still going down on the accelerator and the car in fourth gear. When the police officer walked up to my car, I mistakenly handed him the fake ID I used for drinking instead of my real one. Realizing my mistake, I gave him the real one and explained that "a friend" had left *his* ID in *my* wallet. Would the officer please give it back to me so I could return it to my friend? The officer very politely told me to tell my "friend" he could stop by New Kent County Courthouse to pick up his license.

The officer then instructed me to get out of the car because he thought I had been drinking. I went through the standard field sobriety tests and then blew into the Breathalyzer. Luckily for me, all of my drinking had been done earlier in the day and I only blew a .02. The officer told me he didn't think I was drunk, he just thought I was stupid.

"Last time I looked, being stupid was not an 'arrestable' offense," he said.

He then proceeded to write me a ticket for going 112 in a 65-mile-an-hour zone. Little did that officer know that I also had an ounce of pot in the console next to the driver's seat! Once again I had escaped! Or so I thought.

My ticket said I would have to appear before the judge at the New Kent County Courthouse about three months later. As I made the drive back to New Kent I wasn't worried. I figured this was just another hick county that wanted my money. I didn't even bother to get a lawyer. I planned on going in, listening respectfully to the judge, pleading guilty, and paying the fine.

It turned out the judge had other ideas. He looked at me, looked at my record, and sentenced me to thirty days in jail. He also told me I had to turn in my driver's license for a year. My jaw dropped.

Fortunately, the prosecuting attorney thought the judge's ruling was a bit harsh and he talked "his honor" into lowering my sentence. It was reduced to ten days in jail (weekends only) and a six-month loss of my driver's license. The judge said I could drive straight home now. But I would have to return every Friday and report to the jail.

"Your Honor, how am I supposed to get back here without a driver's license?" I asked.

"Not my problem," he said. "Next case!"

I can report that there is nothing quite like needing your father to drive two and a half hours to drop you off at jail on a Friday afternoon, and then come back on Sunday afternoon, pick you up, and drive another two and a half hours back home, and then do that for four more weekends. My dad was more than a little pissed.

I served my time in a cellblock with six other "weekenders," as we were called. Everyone but me was there for a second DUI offense. Even the guards were surprised that I had been sentenced to jail. I spent most of those five stays playing cards with my fellow offenders, just waiting until I could have my weekends to myself again.

Six months later, I was back behind the wheel. And not much wiser. I couldn't understand why I kept getting speeding tickets. Maybe my cool little green sports car was the culprit. Living and working in Northern Virginia, I had to have a car. But maybe I should be driving something that would slow me down a bit. I traded in the Mitsubishi and bought a bright, almost new, red Jeep Wrangler. Little did I know I would also be trading all the Mitsubishi's reckless driving tickets for a bunch of DUIs.

In May 2000, less than a week after I got my "new" Jeep, I left a bar in Arlington with a friend around 1:00 a.m., jumped in the Wrangler, and took off with the top down and the radio turned up. Not surprisingly, a police cruiser drove up behind me and signaled me to pull over. When the officer came to the driver's side door, he told me he had run the license plate and it came back registered to an Eclipse. (When I purchased the Jeep, the dealer had assured me he would transfer the tags from my Eclipse.) The officer then proceeded to run the Jeep's VIN number, which popped up as a stolen car!

After much discussion with the police officer about my vehicle, I showed him the bill of sale, which was still in the Jeep. That satisfied him that it wasn't stolen. Then the officer asked me to get out of the car and take the standard intoxication tests. Please walk in a straight line. Touch your nose with your index finger. Say your ABCs. Then he gave me a Breathalyzer test. I blew a .16. The officer said my friend could drive my Jeep home. I was arrested and taken to the Arlington County jail. At my request, the police called Steve, the owner of K & E Printing, who came and bailed me out. Three months later, I had to appear in front of a judge—again.

My court appearance was no laughing matter. In Virginia, even a first-time DUI offender found guilty of driving under the influence can face some stiff penalties. DUI is a Class 1 misdemeanor in the state. It carries a maximum fine of $2,500 and up to a year in jail. If convicted, you also lose your driver's license for a year.

On a case-by-case basis, a judge can decide to waive the fine and jail time and order the convicted person to complete the Virginia's Alcohol Safety Action Program (called ASAP, then). The convicted DUI offender is put on probation along with a restricted driver's license. He or she then has fifteen days to report to the local ASAP office where a case manager decides and monitors what kind of education and treatment programs must be completed and makes sure all the probation requirements are met. If they aren't met, the court can reinstate the fines and jail sentences that were originally imposed.

I went to court in August and was convicted of my first DUI. I was given probation on a six-month, suspended jail sentence *as long as* I completed Virginia's ASAP program. One of the requirements was that I had to attend weekly AA meetings while on probation. At that first AA meeting, I was convinced I didn't belong there. For one thing, I was the youngest person in the group by about fifteen years. Plus, I had absolutely no intention of quitting drinking. After all, I didn't have a drinking problem. I could control it.

Man, the things I believed back then! Or wanted to believe!

In fact, I was clueless.

At the AA meeting, we all sat around a table while people talked about their "problems", their "issues", and their "*feelings*". I didn't say a word. I just watched the clock and waited for the meeting to end. It only took that one meeting for me to figure out that for future meetings, I could have other people sign the sheet saying that I had attended the meeting. And that's what I did.

It would be many years before I attended another AA meeting.

Another condition of my probation was that I was supposed to go to ASAP meetings. I think I was assigned to the "Young Offender Program." After attending only one meeting, I was recommended for participation in one of Virginia's drug treatment programs. Fuck all this, I thought. *I* don't have a problem. I never bothered to complete either program.

Through all this, I was still managing to run the production department for K & E Printing. I was lucky enough to have my own set of keys to the building and I spent a lot of time hanging out with some of the older people who worked there. Anything to make the time go by. And just about every night I was out drinking.

Early one morning, I woke up on top of my desk at work. I had no idea when or how I got there. When I walked outside to get into my Jeep, I couldn't find it. I had no memory of where I had been the night before or what I had been doing. A co-worker offered me a ride home to my dad's house so I could shower and change clothes. As we headed down the street, I spotted the Wrangler. As we got closer, I noticed the Jeep's tilt. Both tires on the passenger side were flat and the rims were mangled. I managed to borrow a couple of spare tires and drive the poor thing home.

What kind of story could I come up with this time to explain things to my dad?

A few weeks before, I had told him a tall tale about how the Jeep's front windshield got smashed. The truth was that I had been out at the bars that night and stopped by K & E to smoke some pot before heading home to get a little sleep. When I got inside the building, I realized I had left my pipe in the Jeep. I went back out to get it but, in the rush, I left my keys on my desk. The office door shut behind me and locked. Not only had I locked my keys inside, but the pot was sitting on my desk in full view. All I had was an empty pipe. In a fit of frustration and anger, I punched and broke the windshield. I ended up sleeping in the Jeep until someone showed up for work the next morning and I could get my keys. Hiding my bloody knuckles when I got home, I told my father a softball had hit the windshield.

By this time my dad really didn't know what to do with me. Have you heard the song that goes: "My car was in the front yard, I came in through the window, sleeping with my clothes on"?[i] That was me.

While the Jeep was being repaired, my father was kind enough to let me borrow his truck. I'll never live down what happened next. I drove the truck into D.C. one night for some fun. I was all over town drinking, doing lines of coke, and having a fantastic time. On my way home, I once again hit a curb and blew out one of the truck's tires. I freaked out, abandoned the truck, and jumped in a cab for the long ride back to my father's house in Annandale.

During my night of bar hopping, I had also managed to lose my wallet. When the cab reached my father's house around 4:00 a.m., I had to wake him up so he could pay for my sixty-dollar cab ride home. One look at me and my dad could see I was incoherent and bug-eyed from alcohol and drugs. He didn't have enough cash to pay for my ride, so the cabbie drove the two of us to the nearest ATM. When we finally got home, my father asked about his truck. I told him it was parked in D.C. with a flat tire and I'd get it in the morning. When he asked where it was parked, I said vaguely, "Over by the Mall."

We looked *everywhere* for that truck. For months. My father finally called the D.C. police to report a lost truck. The officer asked, "What do you mean, 'lost'?" "Well. Do you have kids?" my dad asked. The police department didn't keep any files on "lost" vehicles. Three months later, the truck was finally given a ticket and my father got a citation to pay the fine and move the vehicle immediately.

We found the truck parked on First Street, N.E., in between the Russell and Dirkson-Hart Senate Office Buildings (a block away from the U.S. Supreme Court building and the back of the U.S. Capitol) not far from busy Union Station. Even then, before September 11th changed everything, the area was heavily patrolled not only by the D.C. police but also by the U.S. Capitol Police and the U.S. Park Service police. Nowadays, of course, that street is closed to through traffic for security reasons.

I'll never understand why it took three months for my dad's truck to get ticketed.

CHAPTER 9

Scott

Shortly after my Virginia DUI conviction, I was riding in a friend's car when we got pulled over. We were on I-66 in Arlington heading to D.C. to go to Nation, a dance/rave club in Southeast. My friend tossed a package in my lap, and I threw it under my seat. Of course, the police officer searched the car, found the package (under *my* seat), and decided to charge me with felony possession and 35 counts of intent to distribute MDMA (ecstasy); felony possession of cocaine (eight ball); and misdemeanor possession (marijuana).

I kept saying to my friend, "Hey, don't let me go down for this!" But he just sat back, said nothing, and watched me get arrested. I was furious. After all, his stupid ass was the reason we got pulled over in the first place. He had two different license plates on the back of his car! The corner of the one on top was turned up to show the one underneath. What a dumbass! Who has two license plates on the rear of his car and carries around that many drugs?

I didn't know what I was going to do. I was still living with my dad at the time and working my day job at the printing company. But I had also started working in D.C. at Timothy Dean, a fine dining restaurant and bar in the St. Regis, a luxury hotel at 16th and K Streets, N.W., about two blocks from the White House. I was hired as the "bar back"—the bartender's helper. Bar backs clean up the bar area, get ice, wash glasses, and stock beer and wine. Most are apprentices who want to become bartenders themselves. And most are male. Within a week I had moved up to bartending. While I was working the bar at Timothy Dean, there was an older, well-dressed gentleman who always came in for martinis. My fellow workers told me he was an attorney. They said I should talk to him about my legal problem. The next time he came in, I told him about my drug charges. He said he would need $5,000 as a retainer to represent me.

What follows is a good life lesson that I learned a little too late: Never find an attorney in a bar and conduct said business in the bar without seeing his office!

I gave this guy $5,000, all of which I had borrowed from my father, and he disappeared. Someone at the restaurant told me he had gone off his meds. The one piece of legal advice he did give me before taking off with my dad's money was that I should try to get my "friend" to admit on tape that the drugs were his, not mine. Sometime later I heard that my martini-drinking attorney had returned to the St. Regis and locked himself in a room. A SWAT team had to be called in to get his crazy ass out.

But his advice to me wasn't so crazy. I did get my friend on tape admitting that the drugs were his. He already had two drug convictions and was facing strike three, but he still felt really bad about what had happened. While I was trying to figure out what to do next, police detectives were calling me at my dad's house trying to get me to roll over on my supplier. I kept telling them that they had charged the wrong guy, I wasn't a drug dealer, I had no supplier, and I had no information for them. I went back to the attorney who had represented me in my DUI case and paid him $2,500 to represent me for the drug charges. Again, I had to get the money from my father.

My attorney had told me that the tape recording I had of my friend admitting that the drugs were his couldn't be used in court. So now I was sitting in an Arlington County courtroom waiting for my case to be heard, facing a lot of jail time, and wondering how my life had gotten so screwed up. While we were sitting there, the prosecuting attorney came over and tried one last time to get me to flip on the dealer. Once again, I said the drugs weren't mine.

After some more waiting, the District Attorney came over and said he wanted to see my attorney and the prosecuting attorney in private. When my lawyer came back, he told me the D.A. had informed them that my case wouldn't be prosecuted. I was free to go. On the way out, my lawyer asked me who I had talked to. I said no one. The cops had called me a few times, I said, but that was it. To this day I don't know why the case was dropped. Did the crazy, martini-drinking lawyer from Timothy Dean come through after all? Or was it my friend's brother, who was rumored to be some bigwig real estate guy in the area? I never found out.

But some things didn't change. Still on a restricted license from my Virginia DUI conviction, I was pulled over in Georgetown one night. As usual, I was asked to step out of my Jeep and was given the field sobriety tests—say the alphabet, walk in a straight line, and so forth. I was told I had failed the tests and was put in the back seat of the patrol car.

When we got to the station, I was given a Breathalyzer test. I blew a .12 and was taken to a holding cell. I guess it was a slow night because I was the only person there. Eventually, I was allowed to call my father so he could pick me up. Then, an officer said I could sit in the waiting area. I knew by now that I was in enough trouble and being rude or mean to the police wouldn't help. So I laughed and joked around with them until my dad came.

In some ways I was pretty lucky. My restricted Virginia license only allowed me to drive to and from work. But back then, the states had no way to share information. Now they all use the same system. Once again, I got a lawyer and waited for my case to be heard in D.C. Superior Court. While I was waiting, I decided it made sense for me both to leave Virginia and to move into D.C. I had opted myself out of Virginia's drug and alcohol programs. I figured I was still on the state's "offenders" list for that. Plus, I had quit my job at the printing company. If I moved into the city, I wouldn't really need a car to get around. One less opportunity to screw up. I parked my Jeep in my dad's garage for the time being and headed for D.C.

I had found a nice little apartment to rent in the Dupont Circle area on Q Street, N.W., at the corner of 17th Street. As I walked up 17th after work, still wearing my bartending shirt and tie, I was looking forward to spending the first night in my new place. I was enjoying the evening and taking in this new city life. Along the way, two different cars pulled over to the curb and, both times, a guy in the passenger seat tried to pick me up. Yep, I sure wasn't in Kansas anymore. Or even Virginia.

Through all this craziness, I worked hard. And it paid off. I was promoted to bar manager at Timothy Dean! And then I was fired. The two jobs I was now working were *both* in D.C.—day bar at a fine dining restaurant downtown called the Oval Room and nights at the Townhouse Tavern on R Street, N.W., near Dupont Circle. I had also decided to bust my ass studying. I started taking some classes in business management at Strayer University's downtown location.

I didn't realize then the extent to which this decision to move to D.C. would change my life. But I was beginning to learn. Living and working in the city was so different from what I was used to. I soon met other bartenders who lived in the area and became very comfortable in my new life. I liked the fact that we were all different, but each in our own way. This was one of the reasons I came to love D.C. over the years. I learned to accept people for who they were, not what they did or what they drove. Gay, straight, black, white, older, younger. Somehow we could all manage to get along and accept each other.

When I finally went before the judge in D.C. court, I pled guilty to OWI (operating while intoxicated). Once again, I lucked out. D.C. police had never contacted Virginia, and because I was now a legal resident of D.C., the court treated my DUI arrest as a first offense. I was given a thirty-day, suspended jail sentence and one year of probation. All I had to do was come in for drug tests twice a week. Addict that I was, of course I said "okay." After all, I had managed to beat all the drug charges in Virginia. In *my* mind, I had done so well in the Virginia courts that I truly believed no one could touch me here, either. I was also supposed to attend four or five alcohol and drug awareness classes that were held on Saturdays in a building next to the Superior Court. I actually went to all of them.

Life was good. Until it caught up with me. Each night after the Townhouse Tavern closed, around 2:00 a.m. on weeknights, 3:00 a.m. on weekends, five or six of us would get together to drink, smoke pot, and do lines of coke. Sometimes we would stay at Townhouse, or maybe head over to Fox & Hounds on 17th Street, or go back to my apartment. I'd do this even when I knew I had a drug test scheduled for the next morning.

Not surprisingly, when I took the drug tests, I didn't just fail them, I failed them *miserably*. And for just about every substance tested. From day one I failed those drug tests, but I didn't really care.

Scott after a night of partying

I continued to fail D.C.'s drug tests for a good six months before I was sent back to face the judge. And when I went back to court I honestly thought nothing would happen to me. Why would it? I had managed to skate around all my other court issues. But this time was different. I had violated my probation and I was sent to jail for thirty days.

CHAPTER 10

Scott

I was given my own cell. The wardens were afraid something might happen to me because I was the only white guy in the cellblock. I spent the first week detoxing and sleeping a lot. They had given me a drug to help with the detox but it still didn't stop the cold sweats or the fever. Plus, my body hurt so much I could hardly move. At 22, it was the first time I had been sober for a whole week since I turned fourteen.

When I finally felt a little better, I made a few friends with some of the older guys because of my skills on the basketball court. Then I hurt my foot playing basketball and was given painkillers. That made my last few weeks in jail *much* more comfortable. Despite the drugs, I stayed out of trouble and, after serving my thirty days, I was finally about to be released.

Four of us prisoners were let out at the same time. We were all wearing dark blue pants, a light blue shirt and orange slippers. The D.C. jail was in the southeast quadrant of the city and I was living in northwest. I had no money and a long walk to look forward to. But I was free!

As the four of us started walking, a black corvette with tinted windows stopped and the driver motioned us to come over. We looked at each other and our hearts dropped. We had been out of jail less than five minutes and we didn't want any trouble. As we approached the car, the driver said it looked like we just "got out." We all nodded. Then he reached into his pocket and pulled out a huge wad of cash and his gun. He gave each of us twenty bucks to get home. Shit...

I walked up to Pennsylvania Avenue and managed to flag a cab to take me across town.

My first stop? The Fox & Hounds, of course! I needed a beer.

The Fox was my neighborhood bar of choice. In fact, it had become my living room. Because it was just across the street from my apartment, I always knew I could easily stumble home. All the customers, bartenders and servers knew each other. And I knew someone would always buy me a beer. Or I could just run a tab until I made some money to pay it off.

I wish I could say that going to jail scared me straight, but it didn't. It was good to be out of jail and not to have to worry anymore about the courts. I was done with D.C. courts, and as long as I stayed out of Virginia, I wouldn't have any problems there either. Needless to say, I hadn't transferred any information about my Virginia probation to D.C. And I don't think I told Virginia that I had moved. I did know that Virginia had put out a bench warrant for me, but I didn't care. I was never going to step foot in that state again!

Life after jail was going along okay. My motto from Hammerheads extended to my bartending career: I worked hard and partied even harder. It was always the same at every place I bartended. I'd do a good job and rise to the position of bar manager. Then my drinking and drug use would catch up with me, cause tension with management, and I would end up getting fired. But at this point, drinking and using drugs were no longer an option for me. They were a necessity. I couldn't bear to be alone with myself for any length of time. I always needed people around who were just like me and I knew a lot of them. But I had no real friends. When I wasn't behind the bar, my preferred activity was to sit on the other side of it drinking. I was never happy anymore. And blackouts had become an almost nightly thing.

We had our own rules and hours in the bar/restaurant world. When most people were getting up and going to work, we were just heading home. Those of us who worked at bars would generally close up around 2:00 a.m. Then we'd all get together for "after hours," either at one of the bars or at someone's house. It was our own early morning happy hour. It gave us a chance to blow off steam, drink, do drugs, and play poker. You either doubled the money you had made from your shift that night, or you walked home later that morning with twenty bucks in your pocket.

It didn't matter. We all knew we could make our rent by doing a couple of extra shifts, so none of us really cared if we lost everything playing cards. We traded bar tabs for drugs and we *always* had cash. I thought my early twenties rocked! We all believed we could do anything and there would be no consequences. Half the time someone in our group would have to fill in at least a couple of us about what we had done the night before. I *always* needed filling in. But we never judged each other. Anything was acceptable because everyone had been there.

As you can imagine, this life took a toll on my body. Between the liquor and the cocaine, my stomach was a mess and I had perfected the art of throwing up. Most people call it a night when they start to feel sick. When I felt sick I would go to the bathroom, throw up, come back out and start doing more shots. I've always had a pretty weak stomach. The coke made it that much weaker.

Every addict has his or her drug of choice. I enjoyed the downer drugs like pot and alcohol. I used coke because it helped me make it through the long nights of after-hours partying. Plus, and let's be honest, it let me drink more. I didn't do cocaine unless I was drinking and I didn't like to do too much of it. This gave me an advantage over my after-hours crew. I could always stop, go home, go to sleep, wake up, and still have a couple bumps or lines of coke left for the night ahead. Most of my friends would just go on until their coke ran out. Only then would they call it a night.

None of us knew any "normal" people so, of course, we didn't understand them. There were a few people in our group who worked at what we considered "normal" jobs—that is, not in a bar or restaurant. But they drank and used drugs just like the rest of us. We felt like rock stars. We knew all the bartenders around town and they always took good care of us. Because of this fake celebrity status, other people always wanted to hang out with us, too.

By now I considered myself a professional drinker. I never caused problems at a bar, never got loud, just sat, drank, talked and chilled. I have only been banned from drinking at one bar. But that was because I just decided one day to quit instead of showing up for work. I left the management high and dry and I can't blame them for never wanting to see my face there again.

We bartenders drank just as much working behind the bar as we did on our nights off. By now, my days of being a happy drunk were long gone. I would wake up in the morning shaking so bad from my benders that I needed a few drinks just to calm down. I had also lost all my social filters. I had no idea how I was supposed to act in any situation, or who I was supposed to be.

I think a small part of my brain was saying I shouldn't continue down the road I was on. But that little voice didn't have much power. I would firmly tell myself that I was only going to have one beer. Then I would wake up the next morning and not always know where I was or how I got there or what I did the night before. True to form, I usually had twenty bucks left in my pocket along with a couple lines of coke. My solution was to put in as many hours of bartending as possible. I was trying to save myself from myself, but it wasn't working. I became convinced that I wouldn't live to see thirty and I was okay with that.

Despite my feeble attempts at soul searching, I still couldn't figure out why I was always overlooked for any work-related promotion. I knew the bar and restaurant world like the back of my hand. I had bartended or been bar manager at a lot of places. Besides Timothy Dean, Townhouse Tavern and the Oval Room, I had worked at Archibald's/Fast Eddie's, Mondo Sushi, and Trusty's, among others. I had learned all the ins and outs of the business. I knew I was smart, and yet my employment pattern (hired then fired) continued. After a reconfiguring at my current bar left me out, I knew it was time to move on. Again.

CHAPTER 11

Scott

In late 2004 I was sitting at the bar at the Pour House on Pennsylvania Avenue, S.E., just a few blocks from the U.S. Capitol. As usual, I was drinking—and bitching to the bartender, Jay, who was also the manager there. I was telling him how much I hated working the bar at Finn's. Finn McCool's was another popular local tavern a few blocks east on the "Barracks Row" strip of 8th Street. I had worked there for about seven or eight months. The ownership at Finn's was not getting the return on investment they had thought they would. Now they had brought in a consultant who was making all sorts of changes. I wasn't really getting along with the other managers and I felt my days were probably numbered.

I had landed the job at Finn's after I was fired from my job at Townhouse Tavern. The owner of Townhouse had decided to set some new rules. One of them was that the staff could no longer smoke pot at work. Not long after he implemented the rule, he caught me smoking pot in the kitchen. (That is often everybody's go-to place for a toke because the hood system—the enormous exhaust fan located in a commercial kitchen—sucks all the smoke out of the building.) In he walked and out I went.

Shortly after I started working at Finn's, I moved to Capitol Hill. The daily commute by Metro to and from the two-bedroom, basement apartment around 15th and U Streets, N.W. that I had been sharing with a roommate was a bit much. I found a nice little one-bedroom basement flat on 12th Street, S.E., near Lincoln Park—an easy walk to Finn's.

I liked my new apartment, but I had left all of my friends on the other side of D.C. Making new friends on Capitol Hill was turning out to be a challenge. Everyone seemed to have a fulltime day job. Jay was one of the few people I knew who also bartended on the Hill. So when I wasn't working, I hung out at the Pour House a lot.

Jay told me that Joe Englert, the guy who owned the Pour House, was planning to open a bunch of places about a mile away in northeast. He said I should try to get in on one of them. Of course, I knew about Joe Englert. Everyone in DC's bar and restaurant business did.

Englert had come to D.C. in the mid-1980s when the city's night life was limited and its budget in shambles. He began opening clubs and bars that attracted young professionals working in the city. Over the next ten years, he and a number of different partners opened a dozen theme bars and nightspots around town. Many of them were in the area of 14th and U Streets, N.W. Now, I learned from Jay that Englert had set his sights on H Street, NE, a mile north, and had plans to open seven bars.

Joe's first venture was going to be a dive bar called the Argonaut. Jay managed to get me an interview with Mark, who was helping Joe get the place going, and the general manager, who would be running it once it opened. The interview went great and I was offered the job of bar manager. I had no clue what to expect. All I knew was that I needed a change and here was a chance for a fresh start. I took the job. Who knew, if I did well, maybe I could move up and run one of the other bars Joe was planning to open.

CHAPTER 12

❧❧❧❧

Shaaren

My first year at Earlham, I had met another first year named Michael and by the end of senior year we decided to move to Washington, D.C. after graduating. Besides the 1993 March on Washington, I had also been to D.C. for a long weekend while I was in college. I *loved* the city. It was fairly small, it was clean, it was diverse, and it had great public transportation. After growing up in a small white town in New England, I knew I wanted just the opposite for my life now. And, after living in Bogotá, I knew I wanted something a little smaller and more manageable, yet still urban.

I moved to D.C. in 1997. Hello, Chocolate City!

Michael had majored in Economics at Earlham and landed a job at the Bureau of Labor Statistics. I took a job temping and doing office work. That lasted about eight months. Who was I kidding? Children had always been my true calling and I was never going to be happy behind a desk. I found a job taking care of kids at a child development center called "Small Savers," located downtown across the street from the Old Executive Office Building.

The school offered a modified Montessori program for infants through pre-school. It had a parent-run board and was probably one of the best programs in the city. I absolutely loved working there. I'd spend my days at Small Savers and most of my evenings and weekends babysitting for the same families. I worked *hard*. The benefit of working just about all the time in my twenties was that not only was I making extra money, but I wasn't spending it either. I didn't have the time.

In late 1999 and early 2000, Michael and I started looking for a house to buy. At the time, we were living in the Brookland neighborhood of northeast D.C. but I had fallen in love with Capitol Hill. Not just the Victorian architecture of the nineteenth and early twentieth century row houses, but the vibrant colors many residents had painted them. They reminded me of *Mr. Pine's Purple House*, a wonderful children's book that I grew up reading. The book was especially fun in my house because we kids had the same last name as Mr. Pine.

Michael and I agreed that if we couldn't find anything on the Hill that we could afford, we would look in Brookland, where the prices were lower. In October 2000, Michael and I closed on a house on Linden Place, a one-block street on the northeast edge of the Hill close to H Street, NE. H Street was rumored to be just on the brink of a revitalization, and in 2003, Mayor Williams announced the unveiling of a streetcar plan that would connect Minnesota Avenue to Union Station.

The H Street commercial strip began at 2nd Street just behind Union Station[1]. It stretched east for thirteen blocks until it bumped into what was known as the "Starburst Intersection" where H, 15th Street, Bladensburg Road, Maryland Avenue, Benning Road and Florida Avenue all met. The neighborhood was one of Washington's earliest and busiest commercial districts.

Long before that, it was mostly lumberyards and empty fields. It was only after the Civil War ended and Washington's population exploded that H Street and the surrounding area began to grow. New shops and houses sprang up as streetcar lines allowed workers in the central city to live farther away. Now they could hop a streetcar that traveled down H Street, past the Irish neighborhood known as Swampoodle (near where Union Station sits today), through downtown, and ended near the White House.

The working-class neighborhood around H Street grew and thrived. It was a community of people working their way up the economic ladder. African-Americans, Irish-Americans, and others lived together, if not in complete harmony. The neighborhood was no more immune to the racial

---

[1]   Text and historical assistance provided by Tim Krepp

divide than Washington or the nation as a whole, but segregation was cultural, not legally enforced. Downtown department stores were off limits to African-Americans, but many stores along H Street served as a welcome substitute. Separate was hardly equal, but a real African-American corridor was a true asset.

That began to fall apart after World War II. The reasons weren't all negative. Returning soldiers took advantage of several years of enforced savings and bought houses in the suburbs and cars to get them there. The nation was suburbanizing and, for many, H Street became more of a commuting route to the city than a neighborhood. Flight hit the area especially hard when middle-class residents of all races began to identify a suburban "house with a garage" as prosperity.

By the 1960s, the expanding federal government was attracting many newcomers to Washington—to work, if not to live there. During this time, the established, middle-class, African-American neighborhoods in the city prospered. Even after racial segregation became illegal, the mainly black neighborhoods around H Street, as well as Shaw, Columbia Heights, and the area around 14th and U Streets in northwest continued to be centers of African-American commercial life in the city.

Until Thursday, April 4, 1968.

No event, no story, defines H Street like the riots following the assassination of Dr. Martin Luther King, Jr. To this day, both the facts of the tragedy and layers of folklore that have grown weigh heavily upon the area - and will for generations to come.

The details, the recorded history of the riots of Washington are well-documented. After Dr. King was shot, shock spread throughout the nation, of course, but the pain was felt most acutely in African-American communities. After generations of bondage and dashed hopes, a promising glimmer of light had appeared and then been extinguished.

No response was adequate, nothing felt right. People couldn't stay alone, so they left their houses and came together. Crowds formed. They gathered on H Street, they gathered on 7th Street NW, but the epicenter was the corner of 14th and U, near Howard University.

Years of anger, frustration, ignored promises, slights great and small, all boiled up. Historians will debate forever the spark that ignited the bonfire, but there could be no doubt where the fuel came from. In a world that destroyed all options and avenues for advancement, what good was there in restraint? Incoherent rage was made logical by years of injustice.

But when the anger passed, when the fires were put out, when the smoke cleared, only rubble remained on many blocks. The truth was, Washington's neighborhoods were already under attack by the automobile and suburbanization. The riots collapsed the weakened structure.

H Street would never "recover". It could never be the same. But life continues and the people of Washington rebuilt. The neighborhood endured in the face of neglect and crime. Even the ravages of the crack epidemic, a merciless killer that lacked the drama of the riots but took a greater human toll, couldn't entirely kill the neighborhood.

Today, that spirit remains the solid foundation for new growth and energy. Problems persist and new challenges develop, but the history of H Street is there for all to see and share.

With the city promising a revitalization and housing prices being affordable (our house cost $179,000) it was an exciting time to move into the neighborhood. In the year or two following our purchase, many other folks with whom we later became friends (Lyndon & Dea, Kristy & Sam, Dennis & Claude, Nina & Mario, Rich & Kara, Nancy & Jeremiah, Emily & Dan, Stephanie) bought houses on our street.

CHAPTER 13

Scott

The Argonaut took over the building at 1433 H Street, N.E. It was an odd, two-storey, triangular structure at the far end of a block sandwiched between H Street and Maryland Avenue and ending at 15th Street. At its widest end, the structure had entrances from both H and Maryland. At its east end, it narrowed to a prow-shaped angle that had suggested its nautical name.

The place had been a restaurant-bar in one form or another since the 1920s. Ledbetter's Steak and Crab House was its most recent incarnation. Before that, it was the Triangle Lounge. No matter what the name, 1433 H had always been a watering hole for the African-American community that surrounded it. And from the beginning, it had been an integrated business, with its Greek immigrant owners working next to people of color behind the bar and serving those who sat on the other side.

1929. A photo given to us by descendants of those previous owners.

During June and July 2005 I spent all my days helping get the Argonaut up and running. Joe was short on money for the renovation. The Argonaut was a money pit set up to fail from the very beginning. But somehow, by early August, we were ready to open—with no money, a building still falling apart from piss-poor maintenance for decades and, of course, *me* running the bar.

We put a new coat of lime green paint on the outside.[2,ii] Inside, we kept the original pressed-tin ceiling, which we discovered after ripping down a drop ceiling that the previous tenants had installed. We added a mix of mismatched chairs and tables, a collection of nautical knickknacks including model ships and a large diving helmet, and hanging lamps made from old globes. A large, flat-screen TV hung over the bar. Keeping with the nautical theme, we offered a nice selection of rum—Seafarer, Appleton, Plantation, Pyrat, and Sailor Jerry—and the cocktail list featured tropical fruit drinks. We had hired most of the old cooks from Ledbetter's and the kitchen offered catfish sandwiches, Italian sausages, burgers and sweet

---

2   The following text was adapted from Fritz Hahn's August 2005 piece, "Plans to Set The Bar High on H Street NE"

potato fries. The jukebox played Patsy Cline, Prince, and Shaggy, as well as classic rock and classic soul. For better or worse, the Argonaut had set sail.

January 2006. Photo by Elise Bernard

For some reason, good things started to happen. Shortly after the opening, Joe came to me and said the general manager was not going to work out. He asked me if I thought I could handle the job, and offered me sweat equity in the place. I couldn't believe it! My dream back then was to own a beach bar. Although The Argonaut certainly wasn't on the beach, it did have a water theme. I thought we were a perfect fit.

I threw myself into the job. The Argonaut became my life and I managed it as best I could. In those first tough years, it seemed like every day we were on the verge of closing. We struggled to find staff and to pay them and our vendors. Something always needed fixing. I'm not really sure how we made it through. And I don't know why Joe kept floating the Argonaut. There was no smooth sailing. It seemed like we just kept taking on water. But we fought hard to keep from sinking.

I worked every day at Argo doing whatever needed to be done. Then I spent my nights behind the bar to make a few bucks. When the Argonaut first opened, there was very little night life in the area. A customer leaving the place had zero chance of hailing a cab. Hell, cabs wouldn't even come when we called them! In one twelve-month period, there was a shooting in every direction within a block of Argo. Somehow, we fought on and survived.

The few customers we did have during those early days were mostly older, African-American men, who had been quenching their thirst at this location, no matter what it was called, for most of their lives. They would sit around smoking cigars and tell us stories. Mr. Parker, James, LaMonte—we learned a lot from them.

It was an interesting time. Occasionally, some new, younger, white clients would stop in because they were excited for us to be open. I'm not sure if they patronized Ledbetter's before us, so I can imagine that it was an adjustment for the former Ledbetter's customers. But many white customers were afraid to visit. We had to work very hard to convince anyone even to come and check us out.

Despite the divide in those early days between African-American old timers and white newcomers, everybody seemed to get along once they were inside Argo. We were all neighbors.

Through all the early struggles, I was able to hang tough largely because of Joe. I looked up to him and he became my mentor. I had never met anyone who could stay so calm in the middle of all the stress of the restaurant world. His dreams and his vision for H Street literally sucked me in. And it was all because Joe had given me a real ownership stake in the place. I think that if the Argonaut had failed right away, H Street's revitalization would have been set back at least a few more years.

As hard as I was working and as much as I cared about making the Argonaut succeed—for my own sake now as much as for Joe—I was still just a twenty-five-year-old with a serious alcohol and drug problem. As the stress built up, my drinking increased. I thought I had my drug use under control, but I had developed a soft spot for prescription painkillers. A local businessman ran a very lucrative side business selling everything from bootleg DVDs and pot, to any kind of prescription pill you wanted. I had used them before, and in jail, but until this time, they weren't readily available. They were the perfect drug. I could be high and no one would know. So, I was still a mess, just maybe not such an obvious one. Or so I thought.

The reality was that my long-term alcohol and drug use had begun to make me unpredictable. I sometimes felt that everyone was out to get me.

I spent a good deal of my time just trying to prove I deserved the position I had. I found it hard to be assertive with staff in a positive way or to manage my emotions when unexpected problems came up. Under stress, I could become aggressive or depressed. Needless to say, when I exhibited this behavior, it did not endear me to Argo's staff or customers. And most of the time, I didn't like myself very much either.

CHAPTER 14

Shaaren

In June, 2001, Michael and I were married in Maine. My extended family has owned a property on the Maine coast for several generations. The house we were married in was built at the turn of the twentieth century by my great-grandmother's uncle. It was where Alice, the main character in the children's book *Miss Rumphius*, came to settle down. The character is loosely based on my great-grandmother. It was also the perfect place for a wedding. You walked up a rocky path and there, at the top, sat the house overlooking the ocean. Down another path, a few hundred feet away, was the waterfront. My aunt had been married in Maine, and my sister would later choose Maine for her wedding, as well.

I left Small Savers in the fall of 2004 after seven years. My plan was to start graduate school at George Washington University's School of Public Health and Health Sciences that winter. I wanted to get an M.S. in Exercise Physiology and Nutrition. I thought I would use the degree to help kids who were struggling with overweight and obesity. I stayed in the program for a year and a half, but I ended up withdrawing as my personal life started to implode. Looking back, I don't regret not finishing my degree. Years later, while I do still have an interest in the subject, my priorities have changed.

By the summer of 2005, my life had begun to crumble. In fact, I was in the middle of a full-fledged, mid-life crisis. I was miserable and I didn't understand why. I had a wonderful husband and a rewarding career to look forward to. Michael and I both worked hard and we never spent any money. On top of our Linden Place house, we had been able to save enough to buy a rental property near RFK stadium. From the outside, things looked good. And yet, I wasn't happy. My marriage was falling apart mostly because of me.

One of the few bright spots in my life during this time turned out to be just down the street.

My neighbors and I were very excited about the arrival of a new bar and restaurant called the Argonaut. It was the first and only place in our area where you could go just to hang out. For the first time, I met some new friends. Before Argo, most of my D.C. friends were either people I worked with or people who lived on my street.

Having a chance to meet other people who lived in my neighborhood was very appealing to me. I quickly fell in love with the Argonaut. Old and young. Black and white. Hearing and deaf—Gallaudet University was only a few blocks away. We were all together in this one place, shoulder to shoulder at the bar. I was inspired. I'd find reasons to stop by because I loved the staff, the customers, everything about the place.

And I met Scott.

CHAPTER 15

Scott

I met Shaaren when she stopped in shortly after the Argonaut opened. We didn't hit it off right away, but I like to think that my charm and personality soon won her over. We both drank a lot in the beginning. I was also still smoking pot and doing cocaine every once in a while.

The night we met, she had come in with a couple of her neighbors, Dea and Stephanie. I was a very cocky bartender and quick to flirt with and try to charm any group of women. Shaaren saw right through me. At the end of the evening, I offered to walk the three of them home. Shaaren couldn't be bothered. She sped ahead of me and the other two women. Once we reached their block, I gave the two a hug and headed back to Argo. Not a promising start.

Fortunately, Shaaren and her neighbors started spending more time at the bar, which gave Shaaren and me a chance to get to know each other better. She began to accept my juvenile form of flirtation—I threw paper napkins at her—and we began talking and texting.

When we first met, I knew Shaaren was a few years older than I was. I liked her from the beginning, but I was worried that she wouldn't like me if she knew I was younger. So, of course, I lied about my age. I was twenty-five at the time, but I told Shaaren I was twenty-eight. With the wear and tear from all my alcohol and drug use, I probably could have passed for thirty-eight. Unfortunately, it was the first of many lies I told her over the years.

Shaaren and I quickly became best friends. In fact, she was my *only* friend—best or otherwise. She began to spend more and more time at Argo and before long she was working with me as a server and then a bartender. At first, I didn't really like this. I thought at the time she was being taken advantage of, but I loved having her around and, eventually, I got used to the arrangement. Soon, we were virtually inseparable—working together and living together. Shaaren had officially separated from her husband in 2006. She moved out of their row house a few blocks away and into my apartment near Lincoln Park. We had great times together.

Scott and Shaaren working behind the upstairs bar, August 12, 2006.

The Argonaut, on the other hand, was really struggling to take off. It's hard enough to open a bar and restaurant in a prospering location, but Argo was still in a kind of no-man's land, as almost the entire southern side of our block was abandoned. We were constantly fighting to survive. Rocks and bottles were sometimes tossed through the doors and gun violence in the neighborhood continued. There was a lot of anger about the increasing gentrification that was taking place, often fueled by the sense of entitlement that some of the newcomers projected. The bottom line was: We never knew what to expect from one day to the next.

Through all the uncertainty, I worked hard, supported, of course, by a lot of liquid courage. I had to show the world that I could not be stopped. It seemed like every morning I was calling Joe. "You're not going to believe what just happened," I'd say and then tell him about some craziness from the night before. I think that without all the alcohol and drugs I was using at the time, I probably would have been suffering from some sort of stress disorder. Some of the stories I told Joe were hilarious. But some were awful. And they happened all the time.

One night, Shaaren and I were walking back to my apartment after a shift. We had almost made it home when my cell phone rang. The girlfriend of one of our bartenders was asking how much her boyfriend had to drink that night. "Not much," I told her. "Why?"

When she explained, we turned around and headed back toward the Argonaut, which was right around the corner from the girlfriend's house. As we got closer, all we could see were police cars. Our friend and employee had just been shot in the face on his girlfriend's front porch and the force of the gunshot had knocked him through her front door. He was in critical condition, suffering from a gunshot wound to the face and head. An ambulance was taking him to Washington Hospital Center.

Shaaren and I rushed to the hospital and started calling everyone who knew our friend. He was not expected to make it through the night. We stayed at the hospital for as long as I could bear it, given my fear of hospitals. It was the first one I had been in since the time I had spent with my mother when she was dying. Shaaren and I left the hospital the next morning. Although the staff protested, I had to open Argo.

I could never bring myself to go back to the hospital to visit my friend and employee. Thankfully, he didn't die, but he did lose an eye and half of his skull.

On another night, I was cleaning up and talking to a group sitting at the bar. It was right around last call, about 1:30 a.m. One of the guys at the bar said he smelled gas. Then we all smelled gas! I walked out the door to see what was going on. Standing a little ways away on the sidewalk was the guy I had to kick out earlier in the evening because he was high on PCP and wouldn't leave a couple of the women customers alone. Then I looked down and saw that I was standing in a puddle of gasoline that had been poured in front of Argo's door. Then I noticed a trail of gasoline that ran along the side of the building all the way to where the guy was standing. He smiled at me, holding a lit cigar in his hand.

I grabbed my cell phone, opened the bar door, and told everyone to get the hell out. As I was dialing 911, I started after the guy. I followed him from a distance for what seemed like forever. Finally, the police showed up and I gave them a description as best I could. Then I went back and waited some more at Argo for the hazmat team to come and clear the scene so I could go back inside and finish cleaning up. It was 6:00 a.m. before the hazmat team finally left.

Without a doubt, each day was a new and unpredictable adventure. I'm sure many people in my situation would have said, "Fuck this!" But for some reason, Shaaren and I kept at it, working for little or no money. But a lot of booze.

Because Argo often had no customers at all, Shaaren and I had plenty of down time. We would sit by ourselves at the bar for hours waiting for people to come in. Sometimes, it would just be us and one other customer, like Jeff, with whom we passed the time playing Word Whomp. We often sent the kitchen staff home early and there were many nights I would do both the bartending and the cooking—if a customer actually showed up. But I refused to close early, so we just hung out and drank. I sometimes wonder if I would have given up on Argo had I been sober. It was a hard and sometimes scary job and it seemed like we were always teetering on the edge of failure. But drinking helped me suppress all my fears of failing and simply keep at it.

Through these early hard times, I was learning a little about what it takes to run a business. I'm not sure I could have continued at the Argonaut if Shaaren hadn't been by my side. For some reason, she believed in me. We complemented each other. Even though we were complete opposites in so many ways, we did have some similarities. When I was feeling down, she was there to pick me up. When she was down, I could usually comfort her. Until I couldn't.

CHAPTER 16

❧

Shaaren

Scott was charming, funny, attentive, interested in me, and so different from anyone in my "previous" life. We enjoyed being together and spent as much time as possible with each other. It seemed almost like a fairy tale. I was going through a bad time in my life. Scott was the perfect remedy. He made the pain of my failed marriage disappear.

Shaaren and Scott, July 30, 2006.

I'm not exactly sure when things changed, but at some point the Argonaut and Scott became more of a compulsion. I was all in—hook, line and sinker. For better or worse.

For me, the bar world was so *seductive*. Unlike in my former life, nobody worried about drinking too much or smoking too much. Even if your own behavior was completely out of control, there was *always* somebody who was drinking *more*, smoking *more*, doing *more* of something. And not only was it not shameful, it was revered! The bartenders regaled and challenged each other with stories about how wasted they got. I started referring to bar and restaurant industry people as vampires. The life was all-consuming and we rarely saw the sun—unless it was up when we were going home to bed.

At some point I learned that Scott had done cocaine a few times and that he had experimented with other drugs. Of course, I had realized he was a pothead shortly after we met. We'd be hanging out watching TV and all of a sudden he'd be doing bong hits. As a person who had never done drugs, that was extremely shocking to me the first time it happened, but I pretended it wasn't. I didn't want to seem like I was as inexperienced and naïve as I was! I had been around a lot of pot at college. But that was college! This was Real Life. Even though I had always believed that adults could and should make their own decisions about their life and behavior, I felt that in some ways I was violating my own standards of how I wanted *my life* to look. But I liked him. And I wanted him to like me. And who was I to tell him how his life should look? So I'd just sit there while he did bong hit after bong hit.

When we began to settle down, Scott stopped smoking pot. In the beginning I didn't mind the pot, kind of, but as we began to get serious, I told him that I didn't want to go through life being in the same moment with someone, but experiencing totally different things. More than "normal", anyway. This seems benign enough, right? Maybe even reasonable? Even though it didn't seem like it at the time, this was probably the first time I started trying to control his behavior. He also had this other strange habit of spending his day off in a bar. The *whole* day. I had never met anybody else who did that.

In hindsight, it's hard for me not to think: "How could you not see?!" And, of course, it's true that a lot of my "not seeing" was denial. But some of it wasn't. Some of it was ignorance about a subject I knew less than nothing about. Plus, Scott hadn't been healthy since he was 14, so I had no "clean Scott" to compare him to.

I had always been such a hyper rule follower that it simply never occurred to me to do drugs. And, of course, I didn't know much about them either. When Scott would mention doing "K," I had to ask what he was talking about. When he'd explain, I'd say, "Oh, yeah. There's a Law & Order: SVU episode with that in it." I knew so little about this world. It never occurred to me that someone I knew, someone I was beginning to love, would do these things.

I certainly wasn't the pinnacle of health at this time either. I weighed about 100 pounds, didn't eat much and, between my daily runs and walking to GWU and back, I was putting in about twelve miles every day.

Damaged people find damaged people, I guess.

Even though I had never done drugs, I could hold my own with the best of them when it came to drinking. Like just about everyone else, I drank when I was in college. And drinking was definitely a pastime in Bogotá. Now, in this new bar world, I took my cues from Scott. If it was time to do shots, I did shots. I'm not saying that I had no choice in the matter or that it was his fault. I'm saying that I fell into this alcohol-drenched world pretty easily. We'd close the bar at Argo around 2:00 or 3:00 a.m., then stay and drink for hours, walking home together to his place by Lincoln Park long after the sun had come up. Through it all, I always knew that this was just a phase of my life that would end. I figured *everybody* was going through hard times and when they were done, they'd go back to—you know—being *not*-heavy drinkers.

I can't say these early days with Scott were all perfect. He would have his belligerent nights and we got into many stupid, drunken arguments over nothing. But in general, being together was such a nice break from the responsible life I had before we met. And most of the time Scott was still so much fun and seemed so confident. I was used to saving every penny I earned and the way he lived his life—cash in, cash out—while *completely irresponsible,* was new and exciting to me.

It may sound unbelievable, but in the beginning, I had no desire to change Scott. I just liked being around him. I liked feeling special. I liked feeling free from all the rules and responsibilities I had always set for myself. I had never done any drinking in high school, so this was kind of like the teenage rebellion I never really had. It actually felt sort of therapeutic, just what the doctor ordered. Of course, no *actual* doctor in his or her right mind would prescribe binge drinking, but that's the way it felt to me.

I was in a strange, in-between place. I'd lost my old world and, instead of starting over right away with a new life, I was taking some time off. Scott didn't seem to have any real friends and I had lost most of the friends I had when I was married. We were both lonely to the core and we each filled an immense void in the other's life.

CHAPTER 17

Shaaren

About a year into our relationship, I began to notice more about Scott's drinking. I knew a little bit about addicts and addiction, but most of my knowledge had come from being a peer leader in high school. That was a long way from my present situation and, frankly, quite outdated. I was too old for the D.A.R.E program, having grown up mostly during the "Just Say No" campaign, and like many people, I had internalized much of the morality that often surrounds discussions of drug use or alcoholism. The idea that perhaps there is some kind of moral failing involved, not just a disease. So, not only did I not fully understand addiction, but I didn't *want* Scott to be an addict!

I remember e-mailing friends: *August 16, 2006—Any advice for being in love with an alcoholic on a bender? This is the stuff Earlham didn't teach us...*

On the one hand, I knew Scott had a problem. He didn't drink like other people—at least the people I knew. On some level I even realized that he was an alcoholic. But I still couldn't comprehend what that *meant*. I didn't understand that he couldn't just *decide* to stop drinking. On the other hand, it seemed like he was fine most of the time.

In any case, it was too late to bail out. I couldn't hear the very solid suggestion that one person had given me: *"Run, that's my only advice."* I couldn't hear it because...I loved him.

In the fall of 2006, I was able to get a loan and buy out Michael's share of our house on Linden Place. Scott gave up his apartment and we moved into the house. Early in 2007, when D.C. went smoke-free, we both quit smoking (a terrible habit I had picked up when I started working at Argo), cut back on our drinking, and decided to have a baby. Almost from the beginning of our relationship, Scott and I had talked about getting married and having kids. Of course, I couldn't get married until I was officially divorced. After my divorce was final in early March, we picked a day we were both going to be off work (a Tuesday!) in May to get married.

At the end of April, after we got home from celebrating our friends Joe and Carrie's wedding, we found out we were pregnant! We were beyond thrilled.

Scott and I were married at the Montgomery County Courthouse on May 2, 2007. Even though we thought about getting married at the D.C. Courthouse, it wasn't the most attractive building. Plus, I wasn't sure I wanted to be married in the same place where I had just gotten divorced. Our friends and neighbors, Dea and Lyndon, were married at the Montgomery County Courthouse several years before and the ceremony was very nice. My parents and my sister and brother-in-law came for our wedding, as well as Scott's dad and his wife, his brother, and our friends Dea and Lyndon with their new baby, Roli. (A current member of our family always points out that she was there too!)

Scott, Shaaren, Dea, Lyndon, and Roland, May 2, 2007

Scott and I were both so excited when we found out we were pregnant. Even before the good news, Scott had said he would stop drinking along with me during my pregnancy. I really appreciated this offer. I do remember sometimes finding pills in the house while I was pregnant, but Scott always said they were from "before." And, as far as I knew, he wasn't drinking.

Scott and Shaaren, August 4, 2007

Despite our enthusiasm and Scott's support, I had a pretty rough pregnancy. In my second trimester, I was diagnosed with hyperthyroidism. Though not uncommon during pregnancy, it is not normal either. There was no treatment except to monitor me and "the bug" (as we called him or her). I often found myself too exhausted to keep my arms up long enough to rinse the conditioner out of my hair. But with my heart racing, I couldn't sleep either. To make matters worse, the bug was transverse (sideways), so I was in a lot of pain. In fact, I could barely walk for the last two months of my pregnancy because it hurt so badly. I felt very isolated being stuck in bed all the time, but this baby was worth it!

I was quite a sight to see. I looked like a box. And the box kept getting bigger! I gained a lot of weight—and not just because of all the bed rest. For some reason, spinach and broccoli had become revolting to me. Nothing tasted better than fries and mayo. Amazingly, I could still touch my toes at the end of my pregnancy because of Bug's position. But I didn't have much opportunity to show off this new skill because even after my thyroid corrected itself in the last trimester, I was in too much pain to walk very much.

During my pregnancy, Scott and I met a few other couples (Liz and Bill, Granetta and Kevin, and several more) who were also expecting. Plus, all of our neighbors seemed to be pregnant at the same time, too! I think this might have been the first time in his life that Scott had friendships which didn't revolve around drinking or drugs.

There's nothing like being pregnant to make one notice other expectant couples and families. I was always more in-tune with kids, in general, having taken care of so many children, but knowing we were about to have our own baby made us that much more aware that there were so many families on the Hill. We started thinking that if we are going to be a neighborhood place, we needed to embrace all our neighbors, including kids. The Argonaut was struggling and it occurred to Scott that this was an untapped market. Plus, there were no businesses around us and we lacked a happy hour crowd. This could be the perfect way to get some earlier business! He spoke with Joe and they decided the Argonaut should hire a chef and go family friendly.

First, we introduced a kids menu. I remember telling Scott that we'd need another option for a side instead of fries (maybe apples?) because many parents (like me!) would want something healthier for their children. He ignored me and sure enough, when the first kid order came in, it was with a request for fruit or veggies as a side. We also created a "Family Night" where kids under 12 could eat free off the kids menu. Both of these were controversial moves, for sure, in 2007. There weren't that many other family friendly dive bars. Some of our staff would say "I like kids and all, but not at work!" not on board with the new direction we were headed in. Other restaurants thought it was a terrible idea to embrace kids, or to offer a Family Night where kids ate for free. "Why would you do that?" they'd ask. "You should at least charge *something*." We ignored them and moved forward, anyway.

The other huge benefit to going family friendly is that when we had our own baby, we could still have her with us when we were there.

We spent a lot of time thinking about a name for our baby. We knew we wanted the first name to start with "Ar" for the Argonaut, where Scott and I had met and fallen in love. In our searches, we found the name Arav, an Indian (Sanskrit) boy's name meaning "peaceful." If the Bug was a boy, that would be his name, with the nickname "Ravi." And if she was a girl, her name would be Arahv (Ara for short). So, Ara(h)v Scott (Scott was the maiden name of Scott's mother, whom he missed terribly, and his grandmother—the only other Democrat in Scott's family).

My water didn't break in the "television" way with a big gush. In fact, I didn't even fully realize it had broken, but I suspected. Eventually, after all day of Scott trying to convince me, I phoned the on-call doctor at Sibley Hospital in northwest D.C., who told us to come on in. I was so reluctant because I just didn't want to be "that first-time mom" who comes in and isn't actually in labor! Sometime after 7:00 p.m., Scott drove us over to Sibley. They ran the test and confirmed that my water had indeed broken. I was having contractions by then too. Because the baby was positioned sideways, I had been in pain for months. The contractions actually relieved some of the pain. I was immediately given two IV bags and prepped for surgery. (Because of the bug's position, we already knew I would be having a C-section.)

I had a very difficult delivery. Unfortunately, because the baby was "legs up," the obstetrician had nothing to grab hold of to get the Bug out. Not only did they do the traditional horizontal incision, but I needed a vertical incision as well. And because the baby was stuck, creating a vacuum, they had to tear many of my muscles during the delivery.

At 11:57, the doctor finally managed to pull our baby girl, Ara, out by an arm and handed her over to the rest of the team. But I knew something was wrong. The room was silent. I asked my anesthesiologist if everything was okay. She said, "I...think...so," but in a very unconvincing way. Eventually, the room relaxed and I knew everything was okay. I could hear cries! She ended up with some bruises on her arm from being pulled out so dramatically, but I didn't care a bit. She was alive.

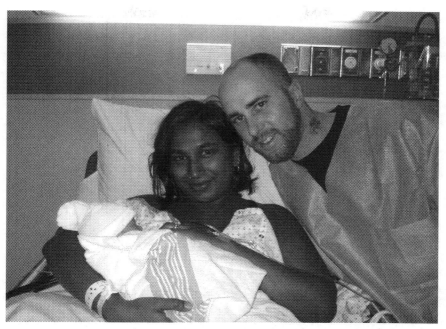

Scott, Shaaren and Arahv Scott Magine, December 16, 2007.

Ara was very tiny, just six pounds. And after losing the normal water weight, she had trouble gaining it back. Because of the trauma of the delivery to my body, I couldn't produce enough milk to feed her. She stayed at five pounds, nine ounces for a long time. After we got home, almost every day for the first two weeks involved a visit for one or both of us to the pediatrician, or the lactation consultant, or the ob-gyn. I wasn't able to walk very well for two months after the delivery either, because every step was re-tearing my abdominal muscles. But I was reluctant to take the painkillers that had been prescribed for me—or even have them in the house—with Scott's habits always in the back of my mind.

Given that I had spent a good chunk of my early life taking care of kids, especially infants, in some ways, my incapacitation after Ara's birth was good. It really gave Scott a chance to be a father. If my recovery had been normal, I know I would have taken over everything. Eventually, when Ara was out of the woods and I began feeling better, things seemed to settle down into a nice routine.

While we did have health insurance, it was crappy, and we left the hospital with a $10,000 bill it took us years to pay off. We had never really had any money and were continuing to make very little money. Scott only took off a couple weeks when she was born because we couldn't afford to not have him work. It was hard to make ends meet just regularly, and then Ara and I both needed a lot of additional and expensive medical attention.

She was my world. Not just in a parenting way, though. I was finally related to somebody! Somebody who not only had my blood and my genes, but who looked like me! She was my first *family*, one of the two people I'd been waiting for my whole life, and I couldn't get enough of her.

Scott was so proud of being a daddy. He absolutely adored his new daughter and loved bringing her to Argo. You could practically see his chest swell with pride. We were both having so much fun being Ara's parents. We didn't really *do* anything with her. In fact, we were too poor to afford much more than diapers and formula. We just enjoyed being around her. In the evenings, we'd bring her over to Argo and have dinner together. From the beginning of her life she was surrounded by "Argo love."

Having taken care of so many other peoples' children, I had absolutely no problem choosing between working somewhere and staying home. I *wanted* to be home with her. How could I have cared for hundreds of infants and then not stay home with my own? It's over in the blink of an eye and I knew I didn't want to miss a moment of Ara's growing up. When Scott and I decided to have a baby, I had stopped waiting tables and bartending at Argo and transitioned to a much more administrative role. I worked on the website, menus, staff manuals, social media, party-planning for both the Argonaut and the catering company we were then running. After Ara was born, I simply continued this work, fitting it in while she was sleeping.

Ara and I loved being together, but I do remember feeling lonely sometimes when Scott was bartending nights and weekends. The weekends were especially hard. Everybody else was with their families and we weren't. Fortunately, since I am something of an introvert, I could usually entertain myself at home. And Ara could, too. And because we had such public lives when we were at Argo, I treasured our home time that much more.

Ara's best friends were the children of the friends Scott and I had met when were all pregnant at the same time. So, from the beginning, our lives were filled with play dates, walks, playgrounds, the library and, of course, dinners at Argo.

As far as I can recall, that first year of parenthood was pretty calm in terms of Scott's and my relationship. But, like anybody with a new baby, the whole thing was kind of a blur for me.

The regular kind of blur. Not the drug-induced-blacked-out kind of blur!

Sure, there were nights that Scott drank too much, but it wasn't that bad. At least in the beginning. But, over the next several years everything went downhill pretty quickly.

He clearly loved us, but was becoming so unpredictable. He was angry and mean all the time. I'd discover open bottles of wine hidden in the closet where our water heater and furnace were. And I'd always catch him in lies about tobacco, about drinking, about pills I'd found in the laundry.

I didn't understand why, if something bothered *me*, he wouldn't just stop doing it! Or, more importantly, why he was doing it in the first place.

He'd mastermind fights and leave the house, slamming the door behind him. He usually returned, and I'd wake up to find him passed out on the couch. Once, in early 2010, I woke up and he still wasn't home. I was frantic and pissed and crazed. If he loved me, how could he do this to me?!

My friend Pam came over and tried to talk me through it. She kept encouraging me to do something to take care of me. It was great advice, but I literally could not pull myself out of the stress and emotion to even contemplate doing such a thing. I'm pretty sure she was the only person I told about it at the time.

On the one hand, how can you tell people that sometimes your husband just doesn't come home without him being judged? Or worse, how can you tell people that sometimes your husband just doesn't come home without being judged *yourself*? And on the other hand, being in the restaurant world, I knew that most of his peers didn't agree with me. He's just blowing off steam, or boys will be boys, they'd say.

For the families, especially families in the restaurant world, there are just so few people to turn to.

St. Patrick's Day 2010, Scott picked a colossal fight with me and went to sleep on the couch. I was still so mad the next morning when I got up that I didn't even really look at him. I just put Ara down next to him, said I was going for a run, and left. When I came back, she was still playing and he had not moved. At the same time I was getting a GChat Instant Message asking if Scott was alright because he had been seen on H Street, looking out of it in the middle of the night. I was horrified as it dawned on me that he wasn't just snoozing. I slapped his face over and over to try and get him to wake up.

I couldn't believe that I had just left my daughter in the care of somebody who was passed out.

I forced him to go to AA meetings after that.

CHAPTER 18

Shaaren

For me, Al-Anon was the only way I could gain the skills I needed to deal with Scott. When I listened to other people's stories about how their loved ones struggled with addiction, it put everything I was going through into perspective. I was learning (and still am) a very important lesson: Keeping the focus on myself was not being selfish, it was the key to saving my sanity.

As part of my Al-Anon work, I started keeping a secret blog. Since I didn't have a sponsor, it wasn't officially "Step Work." But it was a way for me to do my reading and then write out my own thoughts about things. And rant. In Al-Anon, we're not supposed to share all the awful things our addict has done. That's because: (1) everybody has story after story after story, and (2) we're supposed to be working on ourselves. But, for me, writing about the awful things helped me get them off my chest, especially since I didn't want to share the dark realities with my friends.

* * * *

May 24, 2010—I'm trying. Every day (for the most part), I'm doing my readings morning and evening. I'm attending several meetings a week.

I'm not sharing any of my recovery with AH. He sees me reading and he knows I go to meetings, but that's it. Part of me is being vindictive, I think. Why should I help him by giving him any "hints" when I know that he resists doing any sort of work on himself. He's often a cheater—taking the easy road (which is one of the reasons he's ended up in this mess!), and I don't want to help him. And the other reason is I know he wouldn't listen, anyway.

I wish I could say that my motivation for not sharing my recovery is that I know he has to do his own work, but I can't. I'm just being petty.

He says he's stuck on Step 2. [A power greater than myself can restore me to sanity.]

I think he's stuck on Step 1. [I admit I am powerless over alcohol—that my life has become unmanageable.] *I think he hasn't fully admitted his powerlessness—he's still trying to control things. I mean, why keep drugs on you if you think you're NOT powerless? That to me says he thinks he can control his drug use. He used to tell me (with tobacco AND drugs) that he has them to prove that he doesn't need them. Fucking bullshit, I tell you! You know what us non-smokers don't have on us? Cigarettes. You know what us non-drug users don't have on us? Drugs. Fucking bullshit.*

* * * *

In between all the anger and fighting and blaming and denial, Scott would have some good days. At first, the good days outnumbered the bad ones. Maybe there would be just one bad day a week. And then there would be two. As the months passed, there would be three or four bad days every week. Eventually there were only bad days, with maybe a good day thrown in now and then just to confuse us.

These bad days made me feel angry, not compassionate. And I'd focus on him instead of myself. I had cut myself off by deliberately not sharing with anyone what I was going through. In hindsight, that was unproductive. Being strong in my own recovery could only have helped my situation. The longer I stayed focused on Scott's behavior and nagged and yelled, the longer he could pretend his problem was simply that he had an awful, nagging and yelling wife. I should have realized this. But, I was really sick, too.

* * * *

June 2, 2010—When I catch him in something, he gets angry and defensive and throws things in my face and makes it seem like

I'm the one who is insane. Crazymaking. And being sick as well, I start to forget that what I'm feeling is REAL. That what he's done (to himself and to us) is a REAL PROBLEM. So I wrote out my list (mostly my grievances) to validate my feelings. And then I sent it to him. Which, of course, didn't make either of us feel better or help the situation at all. But, like nagging and yelling, it felt like it would be cathartic at the time. Ha!

* * * *

On top of the mental games that are played, being in a relationship with an addict is extremely isolating. I couldn't count on Scott to be my partner, to be dependable, or even just to be the same person *every day*. It made me so sad.

And I said hurtful things, too.

Who wants to admit any of this?

* * * *

June 13, 2010—For whatever reason, I've been really sad since I found the drugs last night—even crying sometimes. Since starting on this road to recovery, I've been doing a decent job of detaching and even though I still get angry (and have a temper and am mean—because I want him to hurt as much as I do!) I haven't been crying about it. But for some reason, this time has really impacted me.

I was feeling really terrible about feeling so sad about it... Shouldn't I be practicing my gratitudes all the time? Shouldn't I be happy all the time? But then I realized I just need to be gentle to myself. That being sad is okay. That I'm allowed to mourn the loss of something—even if it was just the expectation of what a marriage should look like.

Unfortunately, as with today's fight, I didn't say it quite that nicely to him. I'm sure I added "someone better than a fucking junkie" and probably "pathetic waste of time." I can't be sure, but those two things usually come out.

Ah, yes. Well, when I finally reach Step 4 [Make a searching and fearless moral inventory of myself], *at least I'll know what*

> *most of my flaws are! (Especially because I've documented so many of them!)*

* * * *

One of the reasons I felt so isolated was that I was still filled with shame. How could I stay with somebody who was so awful most of the time? My family already didn't like Scott. Why would I want to prove them right by not sticking it out with him and exposing the situation? Plus, in the back of my mind, I thought maybe life with Scott was my penance for treating my ex-husband so poorly. And, if I was honest, I had to admit that I *sort of* knew Scott was an alcoholic that first year we were together. So, wasn't this what I deserved? Even though I didn't necessarily want sympathy, what I really didn't want was to be blamed or have people think that I had asked for this.

In Al-Anon, you learn that addiction is a disease. The brains of addicts literally change as the disease takes over. It's horrible to watch it happen and even more horrible to live with it. It's not exactly like being beaten, although one certainly feels beaten down. But it's nearly impossible for us codependents to share our pain with others because we are so afraid of being judged for loving people who are so very ill.

I had watched shows like "Intervention" yelling at the screen, "Why the frick would she just give him money?!" or "Why would they pay her rent for her?!"

"I certainly don't do *those* things!" I told myself. But still, why wouldn't I be judged just as harshly?

Sometimes, I thought about leaving him. But I wasn't yet at that tipping point. Now I know the goal is not to get to that tipping point. The goal is to find serenity—whether or not the addict is still using. Recovery is supposed to help us save our own sanity.

But getting to serenity is hard. There's no road map. And there's nobody to tell you what the right thing is to do because *there is no right thing.* And it's scary to leave somebody. Having already gone through the pain of a divorce, I wasn't sure I was prepared to do that again.

And I loved Scott. Goddamn it, I loved him.

I think it's easy to forget that part of it for those who are on the outside looking in. Or even for myself, looking back. Scott wasn't a monster every day, just most of them. And through it all we still had this intense love for each other.

Little did I know that our future held something that was certainly capable of moving Scott's addiction off of center stage, and brought us closer as a family, even if only temporarily.

CHAPTER 19

Scott

In 2006, I had used some of the money my maternal grandmother left me in her will to build out the upstairs bar space. I felt that if I just hung on to all the money, I would blow it. Before, all I had were promises for ownership after years of hard work. Investing sped up that timeline and created a little job security. Now, 20% of the Argonaut was mine. And, because I still thought we could make the Argonaut successful, it made sense (to me, anyway) to use all the space we had, both downstairs and up. I knew a lot of people were wondering why I would want to renovate the second floor when we couldn't even get people to come in downstairs. But I believed in Argo and in Joe's larger vision for H Street.

April 8, 2006. Photo by Elise Bernard

I also had begun to think seriously about settling down with Shaaren. So far, alcohol had shaped my life. I knew I was an alcoholic. I had admitted it to lots of people. But basically, with a kind of teenager's mentality, I still thought it was just funny or cool. I figured that having a family would be just the thing to help control my drinking and make me happy. So far, nothing else had worked so this *must* be the answer!

From the beginning, Shaaren never really knew how much I was drinking. She was always wanting us to cut back on our drinking. I held out as long as I could. When we began to think about having a family, I "agreed" to scale back by putting a limit on our drinking: first we limited the shots, then we cut out hard liquor, then we would just drink beer or wine. "Us" limiting our drinking was really just my wife trying to control *my* drinking, and who was she kidding? I didn't do limits. Unbeknownst to Shaaren, I would sneak off to the upstairs bar or go down to the basement where we stored the liquor and do a few shots. I would always lie about what I was doing and I would always get belligerent if anyone dared to question me.

Unfortunately, I was learning that being in a relationship did not bring me the extreme happiness I thought it would. It was hard work hiding all of my defects [defects of character. Program speak for the ways our character have not developed in healthy ways—the root of the mental and emotional part of the disease] every day. But I must have managed to do it a little, though, because Shaaren and I soon decided to get married and have a kid. *This* must be the magical elixir of happiness, I thought.

I knew that a lot of people didn't want us to get married. Shaaren's family didn't like the fact that I was running a bar, didn't have a college degree, and was—by the looks of me—quite unhealthy. A lot of Argo's regulars didn't like me either. Why would they, given my erratic behavior? They thought Shaaren could do much better. But we loved each other and we both wanted to have a baby. I was also trying to find something that would make me grow up, that would magically curb my drinking and drug use. What could be better than marriage and a family!

I had already stopped smoking pot and, when Shaaren got pregnant, I quit drinking, too. That's when I started using painkillers—Vicodin, Percocet, and Oxycontin—on a much more regular basis as a substitute for alcohol. Even though I had begun using painkillers in the summer of 2005, around the time that Argo opened, during Shaaren's pregnancy, I turned this pill usage into quite a habit.

So many people had told Shaaren and me that we would have beautiful babies. And they were right! On December 16, 2007, we were blessed with Ara. Both Shaaren and I had wanted a girl and we were so happy. Now we had our own family.

I loved being a daddy. I was so proud of my beautiful, little, baby girl. Being able to bring her to Argo and show her off, and just being with her (and Shaaren) made me happy.

Ara and I had so much fun together when she was a toddler. She would go to Restaurant Depot (like Costco for restaurants) with me every Saturday morning. Just the two of us. It was our quality time on the weekends since I have always had to work.

As the excitement of being a new daddy finally started wearing off, and our routine set in, so did my drinking. And along with the drinking, the resentment at having to hide things. (I conveniently "forgot" to stop taking the painkillers I had been using as a temporary substitute for alcohol.) I did not want to hide things, but I had promised to quit smoking. I had promised to control my drinking, I had promised to be present. It was apparent that all promises could not be kept. Or any of them, really. As long as I did not smoke around them, or drink in front of them, why should it matter, right? As I tried to hide my drinking and pill use, I attached to Ara. *She* could not be mad at me. *She* understood me. Shaaren was always telling me what to do and how to act. My resentments grew and my short fuse was cut shorter.

Shaaren did not trust me at all, that was for sure. I could not understand why we had to be together all the time. "Why can't I go out with my friends?! I would let *you* go out with *your* friends!" Truth was, I had no friends, and I just wanted to be alone, at a bar, without the responsibilities that came with having a child and being married. And, my definition of "all the time" was skewed, too. I was hardly there!

Shaaren stayed home with Ara during the day and I would go to Argo and work in my office, getting little day-to-day things done. Every day I would come home stressed, checked out, high, smelling like smoke, and trying to talk my way out of why I was stressed, checked out, high, and smelling like smoke. Shaaren would get mad and I found my comfort in Ara, blatantly ignoring Shaaren until it was time to head back to Argo for the night shift. We would all walk back, get everyone set up, start having dinner, and then my nightly drinking would begin while we were there. If I was feeling particularly manipulative, I'd try and find ways to distract Shaaren—either by giving her more wine (so she wouldn't notice how drunk I was) or trying to find somebody else to talk to her so she wouldn't be paying attention to me. Or, I just flat out left them at the table wondering where I had gone.

I constantly disappeared between bars and the basement, creating reasons to leave my family, doing shots and chugging my bottle of vodka that was hidden in the basement. For the most part, I got away with this. Here's the thing about my drinking: when I started, nothing could get in my way. Once I started, going home was not a favorable option for me (we hardly had anything to drink there, that wouldn't be noticed, anyway), and I would always make an excuse or find a way to leave the house. Or, I would just walk out.

I would walk out on my wife and my daughter and drink all night long.

We constantly worked hard as a family at Argo. Ara would be with us, playing or sleeping while Shaaren and I worked, but working in a bar has so many challenges for someone like me. I had spent my life working in a bar, doing the same thing as so many other restaurant people. What was that thing? SHOTS! We would do shots when we were tired, when we were stressed, when customers wanted to do them, and even when we were just bored. This part is not unique to me: this is the way things are in the restaurant industry.

Kid or not, I worked in a bar and I would find ways to do my shots. At first, I could control it, but then I would get that itch and my solution was always a shot.

I probably lasted a year or two in this state, hiding everything. Although there were nights I'd get caught drinking too much or picking fights, I was usually able to fly just under the radar for what was acceptable. And even when I was caught, I was so manipulative and full of promises that by the end of the argument, I'd have Shaaren questioning whether or not I even had a problem.

I hid from everybody the fact that I was now on painkillers all the time. My behavior became very inconsistent. After two separate nights of sneaking out and not coming home and then sneaking out and being passed out at home, Shaaren demanded that I start going to AA.

Even though I knew I had a problem, this made my resentment toward her grow even more. I began going to meetings regularly in the spring of 2010. Things got better for a while and Shaaren was so proud of me. They made such a big deal about my "sobriety" successes that I maybe even felt a little guilty. But not enough to change. So things just got worse and worse.

We spent all of our time at the Argonaut with Ara. Between the lack of sleep, stress of Argo, painkillers and drinking, I don't really remember the details of Ara's first couple of years. The whole thing is a blur. One big blacked out blur.

It's a hard feeling knowing I was there, but not really remembering any events, or anything that happened. I was just going through the motions, but not really seeing anyone or anything. It's a harder feeling knowing that means I wasn't a good father or husband.

CHAPTER 20

Scott & Shaaren

Shaaren

One of my favorite things to do in the summer was to get up early and go for a morning run. There was something about it just beginning to get light and the feeling that nobody else was up that I absolutely adored. I had gotten up and out early my whole life. Even as a teenager on vacation at the family house in Maine (when, arguably, most teenagers were probably sleeping in), I'd get up at dawn and go down to the ocean to hunt for scallop shells.

On Sunday, June 20, 2010, I got up around five thirty or six and left the house for my morning run. I took my usual route: down Linden Place to 12th Street, up 12th to Lincoln Park, then a quick right to 11th and on up to Pennsylvania Avenue. Then down Penn, around the Capitol, and then back home down Maryland Avenue. After I got home and hopped in the shower, all I could hear were sirens that sounded like they were coming from H Street. I tried to rouse a sleepy and grumpy Ara by calling out: "Come to the bathroom window and look at all the fire engines! Something big must have happened!" But she wasn't interested. Scott couldn't have cared less, either, and preferred to stay in bed as long as possible.

Eventually, Scott got up, dressed and left for his early morning AA meeting. On weekends, he usually went to a meeting each morning before going to work at Argo. During the week, he'd go to noon meetings. Ara and I had the whole day in front of us. We were talking about what we wanted to do when the phone rang. I thought it was a little strange when I saw that it was Scott calling. He had only left a few minutes before and, presumably, one didn't make phone calls at AA meetings. I figured he must have forgotten something and I picked up the phone. In a broken voice, Scott told me that the Argonaut had burned down. Then he hung up.

Frantic, I threw on an Argo t-shirt, a pair of shorts and my shoes of choice that summer, Newport Keens, and headed out the door with Ara. Not knowing what had actually happened, it suddenly occurred to me that I maybe shouldn't bring my two-and-a-half-year-old baby to whatever I was about to encounter. I knocked on our next door neighbors' door and asked my very pregnant friend Nancy if she could watch Ara. Then I started running down the south side of H Street, stopping only when I reached the Argonaut. I stayed on the H Street side of the building for a while, not really knowing where to go or what to do. I couldn't find Scott right away, but all the police officers knew who I was and nodded their heads in sympathy.

Scott

I begrudgingly left the house around 7:00 a.m. on June 20, 2010. It may have been Father's Day but I was off to attend what I called my "wife-mandated" AA meeting. The meeting was held in the sanctuary of the Baptist church a few blocks from our house. I liked this particular meeting because there were always a lot of people (usually over a hundred) and I could sneak in and out without worrying about being seen. Like every other weekend morning, I planned to drive by the Argonaut before heading to the meeting. I always wanted to make sure the bartenders had actually *left the place* after their shifts the night before. As I knew from my own experiences of leaving work as the sun was coming up, that wasn't always the case. When I turned the corner from 12th Street onto H, I noticed that the streets ahead were completely blocked off by fire trucks and police cars. I turned around and drove two blocks over to Maryland Avenue. Argo's back entrance and patio faced Maryland and I figured I could go in that way. But once I turned onto Maryland, I could see that it was also blocked. And then I realized why.

Holy shit! The Argonaut was on fire!

The first police officer I ran into was also a neighbor. He said he was just about to come to the house and get me. My worst nightmare had come true. I called Shaaren and told her that the Argonaut had just burned down. Then I hung up. Then I started crying. In the blink of an eye I had lost everything.

I had so many questions. What had happened? How did the fire start? How would we survive? Was everybody okay?

But the police had their own questions. What time did I leave Argo last night? Who else worked that night? What time did they close up? As if the fire wasn't bad enough, I was a suspect. *We all were.*

Much of that day is a blur to me now. Except the smell. I will never forget the smell.

The fire had started in—and completely destroyed—the kitchen. The TVs in the bar area had melted and the roof had started to collapse. But, thankfully, the fire hadn't spread to the rest of the building. The fast response of our local fire department saved us from total destruction. The firefighters had responded to the first fire call in two minutes and fifty-six seconds. We were very lucky they weren't on another call at the time.

Argonaut Fire, June 20, 2010

Shaaren

I could see right away that the Argonaut hadn't "burned down," as Scott had told me. But it was badly damaged, more than I ever could have imagined. I didn't know what to do first. By the time I found Scott, it was clear that he was falling apart. But I was smack dab in the middle of some serious Al-Anon reprogramming. That meant I was determined (1) not to fall apart, (2) to make the absolute best of the situation, and (3) to rally everybody. I don't really know why I was so focused on the rallying part. I wasn't the kind of person who typically did that. But for some reason, crisis mode kicked in and told me that this could not be the last of the Argonaut.

From the beginning, Scott and I had loved Argo because it was the kind of place we'd want to go to if we were going out. And then, somewhere along the way, we became a part of Argo—and it became a part of us. If the Argonaut failed, what would that say about us?

The kitchen was completely destroyed and the bar area was badly charred. The ash and the fire hose water had mixed to create a disgusting paste that covered the floors. Glass was everywhere and everything was melted or sooty. And the smell! I'd never smelled a fire before. It was distinct and horrible and it coated the inside of my nose. It was the smell of things that shouldn't be burned.

The police were milling around and the firefighters continued to knock out windows to vent the smoke and heat. Then, just as suddenly as they had arrived, and maybe with the same urgency, they all left. To go on with their own lives. To answer other 911 calls. To see other people on the worst days of their lives.

We were left to deal with the devastation.

Inside bar looking towards kitchen, June 20, 2010

Inside door of kitchen, looking left, June 20, 2010

Scott

After the initial shock and disbelief wore off, I started assessing the situation. A lot of the wreckage, including the broken-out windows and the holes in the roof, was caused by the firefighters' efforts to contain the blaze. I never realized before that we had twenty windows.

Once the Fire Marshall gave us the all-clear, we started cleaning up the broken glass and debris on the sidewalk. We called our insurance companies and were told we couldn't start the cleanup process until they had completed a full investigation, including an appraisal of damages. Little did we know at the time that the fire investigation would take months.

I'm not sure why, but the fire department had told us not to let anybody take pictures. A couple of people had already come by with cameras. Of course, everybody wants to be the first person with the scoop. I get that. Most people understood when we told them the fire department had requested that no pictures be taken. However, one woman was bullying us about taking some photos to "get the information out there" and "tamp down the rumors." We didn't really know how to handle her. Fortunately, our friend Frank, who owned Sova down the street, dealt with her because we were too emotionally exhausted.

We barely had a chance to think between the time when the fire engines left and the fire engine chasers showed up. These were the companies that cleaned and rebuilt after these kinds of disasters. They were all pressuring us to sign up right away for their services. Our insurance company had recommended that we use Belfor USA. It would do the work and get reimbursed directly by the insurance company. We had no experience dealing with remediation, no crew and, most critically, no money. Our decision that first day to use Belfor for the cleanup and some of the rebuilding made life just a little easier.

Shaaren

Scott and I had pulled up a couple of patio chairs and a table on the Maryland Avenue side of Argo. As we sat there, staff members began arriving for their shifts and patrons came by expecting Sunday brunch.

We told them all about the fire. By now Scott had begun to pull himself together. He called our handyman, Herman, to come board up the window openings. Our friends Liz and Bill had taken over Ara duty from Nancy. Thankfully, with two play dates in a row, our baby got to spend the day blissfully unaware.

Almost immediately, we started worrying about money. Shortly before the fire we had offered a special on one of those daily deals sites ("Spend $20 and receive $45 worth of Argo goodness!"). It was a great success. We had received a large check, which we used to pay off all the debt we had accumulated since Argo's opening in 2005. For the first time, we were professionally debt-free! But we had absolutely no extra cash personally or professionally. And now we had no source of income.

Scott

The rest of that day, Shaaren and I sat outside near the patio. We talked to our staff, our neighbors, and others in the community who had heard the news and stopped by to offer their condolences. We had no idea what an impact this event would have on us.

Once word spread, support started pouring in. That was the first time I realized how lucky we were. Up until then, we had mostly heard complaints about the Argonaut. And it had been hard to separate work and personal life. We would be at the playground as a family, or out for a walk and people would come up to us and tell us how horrible the service was, or how inconsistent the food was, or how much they wished we hadn't changed x, y or z. We never knew just how much the Argonaut meant to so many people. I was always stressed out and bogged down in my own little world. There were always so many bills and so much debt. Most days were a struggle just to get Argo's doors open and take care of our customers. It was hard to imagine that people actually liked us and cared about us.

This was the first time I took a step back and actually saw what we had created. I truly believe all the support we got during the days right after the fire gave me the strength to fight for the Argonaut, to try to bring it back, to stay positive. We were so thankful that all our staff and customers were safe. The fire had started at a time when no one was there so no one was hurt. There was only one way in and out of the kitchen and the electric meter was right next to it. If the kitchen team had been working when the fire started, we, or our team, may not have been so lucky.

In the aftermath of the fire, Shaaren and I reacted in opposite ways. On the day of the fire, I was a mess. She was the level-headed one, yelling at me to pull myself together and set a good example for our staff. As we began the rebuilding process, the roles switched. She became much more emotional and traumatized as the summer wore on.

Shaaren

Early on, as a couple, Scott and I had never had much money. He worked for tips and sporadic paychecks and my own regular paycheck was small. We were able to make ends meet, but that was about it. The fire knocked out that fragile balance. Miraculously, with help from Joe, my parents, and Scott's dad, we were able to keep our house. But we lost our expensive yet terrible health insurance and couldn't pay our bills. I had always been in charge of the bill paying, but when all the envelopes started changing colors, I couldn't deal with it. I turned that responsibility over to Scott.

I was also traumatized by the fire. My fear of fire—and anything to do with electricity or heat—pre-dated Argo's fire. I'm not sure where it came from, but it became significantly greater after our fire. I was even more keenly aware of sirens and fire engines and would sometimes start crying when I heard them. I was like a small child, except panic and anxiety replaced joyful excitement. Every time I heard the first set of sirens from House of Pain (the name our local engine company that responded to Argo's fire had given itself), I'd try to figure out which way they were headed. If I heard a second set coming from the Barracks Row engine company over on 8th Street, S.E., I'd get nervous and assume it must be a really bad fire because one engine company wasn't enough. I didn't realize I was doing this until Nancy pointed it out one day when she caught me staring off into the distance, mentally counting fire engines.

I really don't remember much about Scott's behavior during this time. My trauma over the fire and my anxiety about money pretty much pushed out everything else. Except Ara. We'd play at home or go to the playground or we'd have regular play dates with our friends and neighbors. When we got home, I'd put Ara down for her nap. Then I'd try to catch up on Argo's drastically changed office work while crying as I listened to *Grey's Anatomy* reruns. I'd never watched the show before, and in hindsight I am glad I picked a show I wasn't attached to. To this day, I can't watch it. I stressed myself into my first flare-up of ulcerative colitis during this time.

I think what got me—and Scott—through those early days right after the fire was the response of our community. It rallied around the Argonaut and around us personally. The day of the fire, we started a "fire blog" on Argo's website. We posted pictures of the damage, kept people updated on our progress, and shared the incredible number of e-mails, texts, tweets and in-person responses that flowed in every day. Perhaps most importantly, it gave us a way to thank real people for their very real help and support.

CHAPTER 21

Shaaren

Day 1[3]. *Sunday, June 20, 2011*

We never found out who called 911 early Sunday morning. But because of that call, the fire department got to Argo in time to limit the damage mostly to the kitchen and the bar area. And history was on our side too. Argo's kitchen used to be an alley. The wall separating the kitchen from the bar was originally an exterior wall made up of several layers of brick. That thicker brick wall helped contain the fire. When Scott and I saw the kitchen, it really hit home what the fire fighters had to deal with. I couldn't imagine having to walk inside what surely must have been an inferno.

Everyone who stopped by or contacted us on that first day kept asking what they could do to help. Unfortunately, we really couldn't say. We had to wait for the insurance companies to do their assessments. We couldn't even begin to think about rebuilding. But we begged people to please call the police if they noticed anyone trying to break in, especially at night.

That first day was especially frustrating because we couldn't even take the food out of the kitchen or start cleaning. The fire investigators from our two insurance companies (building and business) along with the city, and the electric company were worried that we'd contaminate the scene before they had a chance to make their assessments. I had never smelled anything so bad. A fire-damaged restaurant, in the middle of summer, with beef,

---

3   This entire chapter has been modified from The Argonaut website.

poultry, seafood, and all sorts of dairy, both raw and cooked, just sitting there rotting. You could smell Argo from a block away.

We were also worried about our restaurant license. Obviously, we wouldn't have a kitchen for a while. That meant we'd probably have to get a new (tavern) license. How long would that take and how difficult would it be?

It was hard to sit still, but I didn't know what to do with my time or energy. We had no control. We just had to wait on the insurance companies. To make matters worse, we learned we were underinsured. Fixing the damage was going to max out both our building and personal property insurance.

Despite all the uncertainty, a few things were actually getting done. All the window openings and the two holes in the roof were boarded up, thanks to our handyman, Herman, and his crew. Mark from the Star and Shamrock two blocks up H Street had let us use his Home Depot card to get some supplies. Patrons from Granville Moore's up the street brought us a round of drinks. And Steve Lambert from Rock & Roll Hotel was already organizing the first fundraiser for Argo.

Scott and I were trying hard to stay optimistic. Argo would turn five in August and we had planned to throw a birthday party. We definitely wanted to be open in time for that.

Day 2. *Monday, June 21*

There's something about the day after that's both worse and better than the actual event. By Monday, we weren't running on adrenaline anymore. Reality had started to sink in—for better or worse. At least we had a loose timeline for putting stuff back together. And we realized that we actually *could* put stuff back together. In fact, it seemed reasonable that we might even be able to open in a month. At least the upstairs and the patio. But it was frustrating that we would have to wait fourteen days for the Fire Incident Report to be issued before we could get the demo permit we needed to start work.

My emotions were both a little rawer and a little more stable than they were on Sunday. On my morning run, I couldn't find a song I wanted to listen to on my iPod. Too sad…Argo memory…etc., etc. But the previous day's tears for what we had lost gave way to tears of gratitude. I always knew how much Argo meant to Scott and me. I just had no idea how much it meant to so many other people.

The outpouring of love and support was overwhelming.

It was what got Scott and me through those first two days. Over 100 tweets and e-mails came in, along with calls, texts, Facebook posts and in-person hugs. They helped us focus on what we had rather than what we had lost.

Day 3. *Tuesday, June 22*

None of us was sleeping very well. Even when I did fall asleep, I'd always wake up in a panic, thinking I smelled smoke or that the house was on fire. Maybe this was a normal reaction. Maybe it was because every time we stepped inside Argo, our clothes, our shoes, our hair, and our skin ended up smelling like smoke.

Tuesday was a big day. Our storage "Pod" and dumpster were delivered. Too bad we couldn't actually use them until the insurance assessment was completed. At this point, both our own electrician and the insurance people seemed, unofficially at least, to think they knew what caused the fire and that we weren't at fault. But the insurance companies wanted a professional "fire restoration team" to come and give an estimate on the costs of the clean-up. They also wanted an independent "Cause of Origin" person to do a separate investigation. We were beginning to realize this was going to take some time.

Some good things were happening. Scott got a call from the Fire Chief. Despite the fact that there were eight other fires the same day as ours, the Chief said he hoped to get us a report by Thursday rather than the original fourteen days we had been told it would take. We needed that report to move forward on any demolition or rebuilding.

We got tremendous support from the community in applying for a temporary tavern license. Our council member, Tommy Wells, and his staff were a great help, along with our neighborhood commissioner and the many friends, neighbors and customers who wrote to the D.C. Alcoholic Beverage Regulation Administration (ABRA) to support the temporary change. When we went to the ABRA office to fill out the application for the tavern license, the staff there showed us the stack of e-mails and phone messages they had received supporting our request. They said they had never seen so many people speak up on behalf of an establishment. The hearing would be the next day and they expected our request to be approved.

Day 4. *Wednesday, June 23*

During these early days, we were always busy but nothing ever seemed to get finished. It was emotionally draining. We'd start on one thing and something else would come up that needed attention. And poor Ara! I'm afraid I applied television more liberally than usual because I had so many things to do. But at least she was enjoying all the extra tube time.

There was some good news. The insurance company's fire investigator gave us the go-ahead to start work on the upstairs cleaning. Our electrician and plumber worked out a plan to get the electricity restored upstairs and fix the leaks in the plumbing. And ABRA granted us a ninety-day tavern license.

Despite the good news, the day was particularly hard for both Scott and me. By early evening, we both felt so…undone. Maybe it was just the accumulation of worry and stress. I had knots in my stomach all day and had to keep reminding myself to breathe. Perhaps it was just painful to see Argo languishing and not be able to do much about it. Maybe it was simply because it was Wednesday.

Over the years, Scott and I were both at the Argonaut four or five days each week. But they weren't always the same days. Except for Wednesdays. We both were *always* there on Wednesdays for "Family Night" (barring the couple of times Ara was sick, or when we went on vacation the previous summer). This Wednesday night, we weren't there. No one was. Scott, Ara and I spent the evening at home. It was nice to relax for a moment. But it was also sad.

Day 5. *Thursday, June 24*

Scott met with the fire restoration people from Belfor. They would be doing our cleanup and needed to come up with an estimate for the work to submit to our insurance company. On Saturday, they would start upstairs and eventually work on the downstairs dining room. They would clean and restore everything. They also thought they'd be able to get the windows fairly soon—a good thing because it was dark and hard to see where the damage was. They also restored hot and cold water upstairs. If all the stars aligned it looked like we might be up and running soon.

That evening, all of our current staff came over to our house. The get-together was supposed to be low-key, but our cook went a little overboard with the food prep and we had a wonderful feast. We were all used to working together during the evening hours, but being together for a purely social event was pretty special.

Day 6. *Friday, June 25*

On the first full day of work, we finished removing everything from the second floor, inventoried all the stuff, emptied all the open booze bottles and tossed all the damaged items into our almost full dumpster. The last of the tables and chairs were washed and put into the Pod.

The two variables that could hold up progress were getting the new windows and the continuing investigations by the D.C. Fire Department, both of our insurance companies, the electric company, and the alarm company. They wouldn't be completed until early July. Only then could we start work on the kitchen.

Day 7. *Saturday, June 26*

Belfor started their cleanup. Wearing masks and remediation suits, they scrubbed, stripped and cleaned. They also fixed the roof. The electricians restored temporary power to part of the upstairs. At the same time, a group of employees, a patron, John, and our neighbors, Robyn and James, cleaned everything that could be salvaged from upstairs, including unopened bottles of alcohol and an old-fashioned diver's mask. Then we struggled to fit all the stuff in the Pod.

We also met with a wonderful neighborhood architect, Gavin Daniels, who had volunteered his firm's help. There wasn't much we could do at the moment. But after the investigations were finished and Belfor could demo the area, he'd be able to help us with plans for the "new" Argo.

In the afternoon, still gross from cleaning, Scott and I took a walk with Ara over to the Ward 6 Family Day celebration at a nearby recreation center. We got there late, but in time to see some of our neighbors. And Ara got her very own firefighter hat, which she proudly wore for the rest of the day.

Day 8. *Sunday, June 27*

All the rotting food finally went in the dumpster. The stench had been getting worse each day. Ara threw up on the patio. I had a stomach of steel and I had almost thrown up on Saturday inside the old bar area. The dumpster would be picked up Monday morning and emptied. Then we could give the whole area a good power wash. That felt like real progress.

Before we left for the day, Scott and I scooped up what was left of the paperwork from what used to be Argo's office. Located directly above the first-floor bar area next to the kitchen where the fire was most intense, it had been totally destroyed. It looked like a hurricane had just come through. We lost a lot of paperwork—everything that showed how much of a struggle the first five years of business had been. Scott had spent much of his time over the years in that office, looking at bills to pick a lucky winner who was going to receive payment that month.

When we got the pile of paperwork home, we dumped it on top of the comforter on our bed so we could organize it. A little too late we discovered that the whole pile was full of tiny shards of glass. We settled down to pick out all the glass so that at least what paperwork was left would be organized whenever Argo got its office back.

Day 9. *Monday, June 28*

The dumpster containing the disgusting "food" was finally picked up. Belfor pulled out all the downstairs dining room furniture and cleaned it. Most of it was salvageable. Our globe artist, Lee Wheeler, had already produced a couple of new globe lights to replace the ones lost in the fire. Because of all the globe donations that had come in, we thought we might be able to put new globe lights throughout Argo. They would be another wonderful reminder of what an amazing community we were part of. Not all the news was so good. It looked like the investigations would drag on far longer than we thought.

Rock & Roll Hotel's fundraiser was just a couple of days away. Quite a few people had asked us if there was some other way they could donate money to help us out if they couldn't attend Wednesday's event. I finally decided to create a PayPal account for people who wanted to donate. Most of our full-time employees had found shifts here and there, thanks to the extended H Street "family" that offered them temporary jobs. Scott and I decided that any money from the fundraiser and donations would go into an Argonaut Employee Fund. We were family, after all, and we were all hurting. Scott and I had briefly thought about looking for temporary jobs to carry us through. But just dealing with Argo had become more than a full-time job. Joe helped us cover some payroll and supply costs and keep our momentum going.

It was humbling to be in this position. One of the phrases that helped us a lot during the first week after the fire was: "Adversity doesn't build character, it reveals it." What our adversity revealed was the character and kindness and generosity of our community. This time also made me grateful for Scott. I was proud of all the changes he had made in his life. If this misfortune had happened a couple of months earlier, neither he nor I would have reacted in the same way. I'm not sure we (Argo or us) would have made it[4].

Day 10. *Tuesday, June 29*

Belfor finally spray-sealed the walls upstairs in preparation for painting. The dining room cleaning was almost finished. The structural engineer concluded that there was no real damage to the joists or load-bearing beams. We were optimistic that our building insurance would cover all of the rebuild. And it now looked like the investigations meeting with the powers that be would take place on Friday.

Scott was feeling better about things in general and our insurance coverage. I, on the other hand, felt even more overwhelmed about Argo's finances (and our own) and was just hoping we could open soon. Waiting for the investigation reports was especially hard. Even though I knew we weren't at fault, I felt like the kid in trouble waiting outside the principal's office. Behind the closed door, everybody else (principal, teachers, and parents) was deciding what to do.

Our fundraiser was the next day. Rock & Roll Hotel, the host, was providing complimentary cocktails. We would be selling fish tacos, sweet

---

[4]   Scott had stopped drinking so easily, it seemed, and his whole personality changed. He was much easier to be around, much calmer. He even seemed proud of himself – which he had every right to be. He told me he was going to AA meetings most days. I didn't know for sure because there was so much going on. But I needed to believe him.

potato fries and some other Argo classics. We were also bringing along some Argo merchandise to sell (t-shirts, shot glasses, coffee mugs—whatever wasn't damaged in the fire). Some of our staff were coming over to our house in the evening to figure out who would be doing what for the benefit. I still had to inventory our merchandise and make cards for the silent auction. So many people had donated great things for the auction.

Day 11. *Wednesday, June 30*

The benefit was amazing.

Based on the Facebook RSVPs, we were expecting between 150 and 200 people. Over 300 showed up, including the folks from Belfor. Our host for the benefit, R & R's booking agent Steve Lambert, and the bartenders did a terrific job. Our own front-of-the-house staff rocked the merchandise and food tables. The back-of-the-house staff created wonderful food in an unfamiliar kitchen. And I couldn't believe that all of Argo's DJs were there spinning. I never had the chance to hear any of them spin because of Ara's early bedtime. The DJs were already planning another benefit for the Argonaut in early July. The silent auction was a great success as well. Two days before the benefit, we had only six items. By auction night, there were over forty.

Between the auction donations, PayPal, and merchandise and food sales, we netted almost $10,000. We really didn't know how to express our thanks except to keep telling everyone how much their support was helping our staff do things like buy food, keep their housing, take their kids to the doctor, and a lot more.

Day 12. *Thursday, July 1*

The morning after the fundraiser, Scott, Ara, and I went to the bank. Normally, our whole family didn't do that together. But this time it seemed like a pretty big thing. We opened an employee account so that all our full-time employees could request money to help with their housing, grocery, and health care expenses. Plus, there was a huge saltwater fish tank at the bank that was fairly mesmerizing—especially to the smallest depositor in our group.

Day 13. *Friday, July 2*

Painting started today—a major breakthrough. We had chosen dark blue for the walls and grey for the ceiling and trim. Scott also met with Sean Hennessey, who had volunteered to do some decorative painting. We were thinking something small, but apparently Sean had bigger ideas.

The investigations meeting didn't happen but we got our first request for money. One of our employees was having problems paying his rent. He called Scott, desperately looking for the phone number for one of the establishments that was offering shifts to our workers. Scott texted me for the establishment's number. My first response was: "Um, hello? Write him a check! Isn't that what the money is for?!" Scott said, "Oh, yeah." That was our first chance to put the money so generously donated where it needed to go.

Day 14. *Saturday, July 3*

When Scott walked into Argo in the morning, he discovered that we'd been burglarized. Until now, the criminal element had only stolen a cooler, some umbrellas, and a few other small things from outside. And, so far, they had only *attempted* to break in. But sometime during the night or early morning, they pushed in the air conditioning unit. They broke the gumball machine and stole all the quarters; opened the downstairs jukebox to get cash from the collection box (all the cash had been removed right after the fire); and looked in all the downstairs bar cabinets.

The police said there were a lot of good prints that they would hand off to the FBI. They seemed confident they would get a hit because a lot of these crimes were committed by the same offenders. We were just thankful that there was nothing much to steal…and that the person was looking for money, not looking to vandalize the place. The police said they'd send more units around at night.

Day 17. *Tuesday, July 6*

Before the fire, one of my biggest fears was that our house (or the Argonaut) would catch fire. I didn't understand where that fear came from. It certainly wasn't rational. Then, after the fire, I kept thinking, "My worst fear happened and we're all going to be okay."

Something woke me up very early in the morning. I got up and looked out the bathroom window. It was still dark outside, but I could see a bunch of fire trucks…again. This time, they were in the parking lot of H Street's AutoZone, just behind our house. Then I heard about Pepco's underground cable fires and exploding manhole covers.

None of this did much to ease my fire fears.

On the bright side, Belfor finished painting upstairs and started to install our new floors. The kitchen equipment people came to assess our burned equipment—not salvageable. They would be working up an estimate for a new kitchen. Scott started putting up some shelving in the office and was actually able to do some work there. And more money went out—to our employees who had been helping with cleaning and to those having trouble making ends meet.

Slowly, we were getting back some sense of control and getting used to this new normal. Even Ara adjusted. We were so busy in the days after the fire that Ara and I only went to the playground a couple of times. Ara was never a fan of stroller walks that didn't end up somewhere—like the playground or the library. Now we had a new mission. I explained to her that people had bought t-shirts and mugs and shot glasses and auction stuff to help Argo. Now we had to deliver them.

Off I went, on foot, pushing Ara in a stroller loaded with our deliveries. It was a new experience. Despite having lived in the area for ten years, there were so many streets I had never been on. In our regular life, we only went to five places: the library, Argo, and the three closest playgrounds. Even my running route was the same every day. Now, on our delivery walks, Ara and I got to see cool streets where people I knew from Argo actually lived. It was nice putting names to faces and faces to places. An unexpected benefit of the fire.

Day 18. *Wednesday, July 7*

It looked like we might be able to open in a week. Now we had to figure out how everything was going to work once we were open. Besides the damage to floors and windows from the fire, the major loss for the front of the house was our computer system. We had borrowed money to buy the previously owned system two years earlier for about $25,000. It was beautiful and incredibly useful. Orders could go directly to the kitchen or bartender. Staff could clock in and out on it. We could track how items were selling.

Clearly, we couldn't replace it. So, with money from the sale of Argo merchandise, we went to Staples and bought two simple cash registers for $200 each, one for downstairs and one for upstairs. And time cards for our staff. It was back to basics at Argo.

Day 19. *Thursday, July 8*

Ara and I stopped by Argo in the morning to take a look at the newly installed hardwood floor upstairs. Along with the new paint job, the space looked great. The electricians were still working like crazy rewiring the entire upstairs and installing fire/heat/smoke sensors.

Scott went to Restaurant Depot and bought a Panini press on sale. And we put out a call to anyone who might have a George Forman-type grill or sandwich press that was collecting dust.

We would be heading out that night for our second fundraiser at Palace of Wonders—a long, narrow, funky bar a couple of blocks up from us on H Street that featured burlesque and freak shows. We planned on taking some t-shirts, mugs, and shot glasses with us, in case anybody was still interested.

Day 20. *Friday, July 9*

The benefit at Palace of Wonders raised $700 in cash and online donations were still coming in. Like all the other donations we had received so far, they enabled us to give our staff some stability until we were able to open. Scott and I got some stability support too. Our building insurance company informed us that they would be cutting a mortgage check for Argo.

Sean Hennessey and Beth Baldwin, the artists who were donating their decorative painting skills, began painting. Sean had shown us some sketches and equally intriguing descriptions of what he had in mind: "the smaller [space]…lost treasure basically…a background of purple/gold…metal coins…a ship. The larger piece is a map on yellowish old parchment paper, a little torn and burned in spots…mostly earth tones

with a ship in the immediate foreground ('we're all in the same boat'...
kind of thing)...a boat, ropes, some skull/crossbones, etc...I've based the
map on old renditions so it's a bit inaccurate and I think a bit more fun
that way."

Day 21. *Saturday, July 10*

Later in the day, Scott described the latest in our string of bad luck to
anyone who would listen:

"I drove over to our bank to deposit the $700 from the Palace of
Wonders benefit. I made a quick stop first at the Starburst CVS to pick
up Shaaren's prescription for her ulcerative colitis. I was in CVS for less
than five minutes. I left the store and headed back to my car. Then my
jaw dropped. The car was gone. It had been stolen around 10:00 a.m. on
a busy Saturday morning. Inside the car was $700 in cash along with a
check for $20,000 from our insurance company. I called the police. About
an hour later I learned that they had spotted the car on Florida Avenue and
gave chase. The driver wrecked the car by driving it into a wall and a tree
in somebody's back yard and then ran. The suspect had not been caught
and the cash was gone. Luckily, the insurance check was still in the car."

Day 22. *Sunday, July 11*

Three days to go until our "grand" reopening and there was still so
much to do...and worry about. How much food to prep? What if we ran
out? What if nobody came? What if the power went out? What if...What
if...What if?

That night, I worked on our first non-kitchen menu. We decided on
one soup, one salad, two appetizers, five sandwiches, and one kid option.
A generous donation of a Cuisinart Griddler and a blender put us in an
even better position.

Day 23. *Monday, July 12*

Lots of last minute loose ends were getting tied up. Capitol Amusement
was reinstalling the jukebox and it looked like they would be finished with
the new wiring by the next day. After speaking with our business insurance

company's adjuster, Scott was preparing invoices for all the products we lost in the fire. We crossed our fingers hoping the insurance company would decide to reimburse us. There was still no investigations meeting in sight. Scott called the Fire Inspector to ask when we could expect to get a copy of the Fire Report. Apparently, they couldn't release it until the investigations meeting—whenever that would be.

Day 24. *Tuesday, July 13*

The opening would happen tomorrow—if the electricians and the painters and the construction guys could finish. We were hoping to open both the upstairs and the patio. Of course, it looked like rain. So maybe we'd just be opening the upstairs. Or maybe the new umbrellas we ordered would arrive. The produce Scott ordered would be delivered in the afternoon. Antoine was going to Restaurant Depot to pick up the other stuff we needed. Hector and Noris were ready to start prepping. Teddy from Granville Moore's up the street had graciously offered his services. He would be helping our kitchen staff do the prep work at Rock & Roll Hotel's kitchen.

At a staff meeting in the evening we went over how we could make everything run as smoothly as possible. We were just hoping that everyone would stop by, enjoy some beer, and bear with us on everything else.

We were treating the next day as a "soft" reopening. Maybe not even soft. Maybe squishy.

Day 25. *Wednesday, July 14*

As the opening time of 5:00 p.m. got closer, I became more and more emotional. And not just because we were finally opening. I was thinking about all the people who had helped and supported us during this hard time. With e-mails and tweets and phone calls and letters. With donations of money and things and services.

It was hard to explain how all this support made us feel. Lucky. Grateful. Like we had the most supportive extended family in the whole world. There had been bad days for sure, but it was pretty hard to feel sorry for yourself for very long when hundreds of people were cheering you on. We had gained so much more than we lost. In the beginning, whenever

I talked or wrote about "our" Argonaut, "our" always meant those of us who worked there. The fire and its aftermath changed that. Clearly, the Argonaut belonged to everyone who came there. Nervous or not, we couldn't wait to welcome them back.

CHAPTER 22

Scott

Only one word could describe what it was like opening the Argonaut for the first time since the fire: clusterfuck. My office had been turned into a makeshift kitchen with a sandwich press and a prep table. The upstairs bar was functional, but we had no bottle cooler, so we set up a beer tub, ordered ice because we didn't have an ice machine yet, and put all the beers on ice. Basically, it was like prepping for a huge house party.

Our staff did the best they could given what they had to work with. The upstairs space was usable, but the patio was the key. People liked sitting outside. It had taken a full day to get everything ready, and, under the circumstances, we did a pretty good job. The neighborhood came out and supported us and we had a good first night. But with the addition of so many new places to eat and drink on H Street, we knew it would be hard to keep people coming back to our half-finished establishment.

The days that followed the reopening were a struggle. We continued to use Rock & Roll's kitchen to prep cold food items and teamed up with food trucks on the weekends. They'd park on the street outside Argo and we'd allow our customers to eat their food and drink our alcohol. Our large patio was a lifesaver.

Since we couldn't even begin to rebuild Argo's downstairs until the fire investigation was completed, we had plenty of time to think about what we wanted. It was an unforeseen opportunity to make changes. We knew from experience what worked with the existing layout—and what didn't.

We knew we could make Argo better. It was the silver lining after the fire. And we latched on to it to keep us going.

Eventually, the fire investigation did end. With everybody and their lawyers present, we were cleared of any wrongdoing. The fire had started in the housing of our electric meter. Most electric meters in D.C. are located on the outside of buildings for ease in servicing. Argo's meter was on the wall in our kitchen, which had originally been an outside alley. Pepco—D.C.'s electric company—had replaced the meter earlier in the year and it was their lock on the meter housing. We also knew that Pepco had upgraded many of the power lines along H Street. During the summer heat wave, the new lines had some problems and there were a number of power surges along the H Street corridor. We thought Argo's fire was probably caused by the first of those power surges. Once the fire investigation report was issued and we were cleared, our insurance companies turned their sights on our electrician and the lawsuits continued. Fortunately, they no longer involved us. The final determination by the Fire Investigator was that no one was at fault. Unfortunately, the lawsuits (insurance companies, electrician, electric company) continue to this day.

In some ways, our current situation—a half rebuilt Argo struggling to stay open and survive—was harder to deal with than the early days in June right after the fire. During that first month after the fire, my life was extremely busy. I was driven to bring the Argonaut back. But it was a day job. I would work very hard during the day and then Shaaren, Ara and I would be home together in the evening. I think this helped lessen the stress of our situation. One thing about restaurant life—it's a twenty-four-hour-a-day, seven-days-a-week job. While Argo was closed, my new schedule had helped keep me from burning out too quickly. The new focus took away the temptation to drink, and not being surrounded by alcohol probably helped, too. I was still attending daily AA meetings, but I was hiding my pill use. Painkillers were easy to get and helped me mellow out. At least, that's what I thought.

After Argo reopened on July 14, the rebuilding continued, but very slowly. During the whole process, I still wasn't drinking. But I started popping more and more pills. I was depressed. Before the fire, we had very little money and just managed to make ends meet. Now we had nothing and were really struggling to pay our bills. It took three weeks just to get the upstairs bar open. Summer turned into fall. We kept pushing Belfor to hurry up and finish. I called and e-mailed and begged them to come in and complete the job, but Argo just sat there.

We had brought back some of our staff after the July reopening, but it became obvious that we couldn't support Argo (and our workers) in its current state. We had used up all of the cash flow from the insurance companies, we couldn't make payroll, and the build-out was costing more than expected. Shaaren and I had no income coming in and could barely make the mortgage payments on our house. I finally broke down and asked my father for a loan to help us pay some staff and finish Argo's basic punch list.

By December, business had hit an all-time low. Shortly before Christmas, we went ahead and closed the place up. In hindsight, it was a decision we should have made a lot earlier. But we had been committed to staying open so our staff would have a place to work and some income.

Despite our current situation, we were awarded a "Hilly" for Best Bar by the community via CHAMPS (Capitol Hill's Chamber of Commerce) during their Hilly Awards! And the next month, we were also presented with a "Brickie" from our Ward 6 Council Member, Tommy Wells, in recognition for the ways that we helped make our neighborhood more "liveable and walkable". Winning these two honors, in our darkest hour, when we needed it most, gave us a lot of strength to keep going.

Scott, Shaaren and Ara with our Hilly and Brickie awards, December 12, 2010

We had been planning to take a break and visit Shaaren's parents in Massachusetts for the holidays. Originally, we thought we'd come back right after Christmas and finish getting "the new and improved Argo" ready for a grand New Year's Eve reopening to welcome in 2011. Around December 20, when all the rebuild work had ground to a halt, we left for Massachusetts. It was good to get away and it gave Shaaren and me time to take a good look at our staffing needs and to post ads and set up interviews for new hires.

As Christmas day approached, so did a huge Nor'easter. We had planned to leave on December 26 after celebrating Boxing Day with Shaaren's extended family in Ipswich. Now, the whole East Coast was supposed to get over a foot of snow. I watched the progress of the storm on TV and decided that we needed to head back to DC on Christmas Day. The last thing I wanted was to get stuck in Massachusetts and not be able to get back and work on reopening Argo. This was not a popular choice with Shaaren or Ara, but I felt it was the right one. The storm ended up missing D.C., but the I-95 corridor was crushed with twelve inches of snow. If we had stayed in Massachusetts, we would have been stuck.

The break was just what I had needed to regroup and now I threw myself into getting the Argonaut ready to reopen. Even before we left for Massachusetts, we had started doing a lot of the finish work ourselves. Belfor had gone to work on other jobs and kept pushing ours to the back of the line. But no matter how hard we worked, it soon became obvious that there was no way Argo could be ready for New Year's Eve. What I thought was the worst year of my life ended with more of a whimper than a bang. Shaaren and I went to sleep before the ball even started to drop in Times Square.

Little did I know what I had to look forward to in 2011. It was probably better that way.

By early January, we had finished most of the rebuild and the new Argo had taken shape. Downstairs, the whole layout had changed. We put in a steel header so we could take out the load-bearing wall between the old bar and dining areas. We opened up the kitchen and reconfigured it to give a better flow. Where the old bar had been, using boards from the old floor, we built a kitchen service counter so the servers had a dedicated area.

But the biggest change by far was Argo's new bar. The bar was completely rebuilt in the curved shape of a ship's hull—an ancient Greek ship, we liked to think. It stood at the far corner of the dining room with its prow facing the Starburst Intersection.

Argonaut's new bar, January 17, 2011

The bar stools faced enlarged windows behind the bar that looked out onto the patio and Maryland Avenue. The windows operated on pulleys and could be propped open during nice weather. An outside bar was added to the base of the windows. Along with the huge bar upgrade, we built a walk-in—an enormous refrigerator that one is able to walk into—in the basement and ran draft lines to both bars. Our old bar had been limited to four drafts downstairs, and no drafts upstairs. Now we could have twelve, which we decided would be American craft beers from small breweries. And they would be delivered, upstairs and down, through beautiful antique draught towers.

We had made personnel changes as well. Our staff would more than double in size and in the warmer months when the patio was open, we'd be employing close to fifty people. Training new staff was hard enough, but we were also having problems with our old managers. We figured it wouldn't be long before we had to replace them. Thankfully, one of our new managers, Chad, was ready for the challenge.

Despite the glitches, Argo's grand reopening on January 15 was a huge success. It seemed like everyone was there and they were very pleased with the changes we had made. Business boomed and we did close to 50% more in sales than our projections. As successful as it was, however, Argo's reopening had a downside for me. There was added stress and huge new debts (almost $100,000).

Before long, besides popping pills, I started drinking again. I'd go down to Argo's basement and chug vodka straight from the bottle.

CHAPTER 23

Scott

Shaaren was pushing me to see a shrink. She had done this several times in the past, and each time I couldn't understand why she thought I needed one. Or what she thought was so bad about my behavior. In fact, I thought she should feel lucky that I was being so good. In my own mind, I would always compare my current self to the "me" of the really bad years—my late teens and early twenties. That way, I could convince myself that my current alcohol and drug use weren't that bad. After all, I wasn't smoking pot all day long anymore. And I hadn't used cocaine or any other drugs since I turned twenty-five. What was her problem with my prescription painkillers? Of course, I had no prescription for these prescription painkillers. But what I did have was an endless supply.

To get Shaaren off my back, I did see a shrink. Actually, I went through a few shrinks over the years. I would feed each of them certain information and lie about everything else. I was already so shut off from the world that I refused to let anyone get close to me. I sure as hell wasn't going to let a shrink in. During therapy sessions, I lied about my drug use and directed most of the conversation toward my "former" drinking and what I was convinced was the real problem: my wife. I left out the fact that I was now taking painkillers all the time, and drinking, too.

I told shrink number three that I thought I might have ADHD and shared with her my lack of focus and short attention span. I had always known I had ADHD, but I started smoking pot at such an early age that it hid the symptoms. Now that I wasn't smoking pot anymore, those symptoms were starting to show up again. I loved my new and official ADHD diagnosis *and* the prescription that came with it!

Lucky me, I got to abuse both regular and extended release because of my long work day. I should never have been given it, but I was very good at shifting the focus of any conversation, including my talks with the shrink. On top of forgetting to mention to her that I was already taking prescription painkillers and drinking, I neglected to add that I had been a cocaine user. Another red flag for sure!

I was in heaven. I had just been given a prescription for a legal form of Speed! Thus began my downward spiral.

CHAPTER 24

Scott

Breakfast became two painkillers and 20 milligrams of Adderall. The Adderall made me tense and my chest was tight all the time. That led to another legal prescription for Klonopin to take the edge off. That led me back to the alcohol because, in order to fall asleep, I had to drink enough to pass out. All of these "meds"—legally prescribed or not—took a huge toll on me both physically and mentally. My life quickly became unmanageable. Once again, I was deteriorating. But this time, I had a wife, a daughter, a house, and a business to run. I was failing with all of them. And everything I tried to help me clean up my act just made it worse.

I'm not sure how to describe what these constant cravings were like. For starters, they were uncontrollable. If I took one drink, my eyes seemed to widen and it was *on*. From that moment, nothing could get in my way. The only thing I wanted was to belly up to a bar, any bar, and drink. Once I started drinking, I wanted the buzz instantly. That need made me drink faster and harder. And I would drink until I couldn't drink any more. By the time everything hit, I was way beyond drunk. People thought I was joking when I said one beer leads me to a bottle of Jameson, but it was the truth. One beer was a tease for me. I couldn't stop after that. This was just how my brain worked.

I wished I was normal. I wished I could just enjoy a beer like most people did. I honestly didn't understand how people could drink just one beer. Or how they could ever leave a restaurant with a glass half full of beer on their table. To me, *that* was alcohol abuse!

With this latest spiral, I again started closing myself off from the world around me—both personally and professionally. My huge resentments toward my wife, both real and imagined, came back. At night I would sneak out of the house to drink. I would go to Argo, start drinking and hang out with customers or staff for a while. Then I would continue drinking at The Pug, another local bar on H Street. Shaaren usually didn't even know I was gone because, by this time, I had been relegated to sleeping on the couch.

I was a thirty-two-year-old man sneaking out of his own house like some guilty teenager. A rage built up in me. I couldn't control my own life so I tried to control everything and everyone else. And when I couldn't, I would flip out. My family, the employees at Argo, and even some customers would walk on eggshells around me wondering which Scott would show up on any given day.

There were times when I was relatively happy and I would joke around with Argo's staff and customers. But other times, the smallest thing would set me off. Our employees never knew if I was just playing around with them or if I was serious. When something didn't get done I'd explode. Or, I would get pissed off, go ahead and do the job myself, but scream and cuss the whole time. Why couldn't anybody do anything right? I felt compelled to work eighty hours a week because I didn't trust anyone else to do anything. And yet, I couldn't understand why no one was willing to help out. The fact was, I needed to work that much so I could blame everybody else and be angry at their incompetence. It was a way to justify my addiction–induced temper tantrums and continue to feel that I "deserved" to drink and use drugs in the first place.

And, just like when I was younger, I was manipulative. I had never learned to take responsibility for anything, so my only skill in this situation was using empty gestures to get back into somebody's good graces. I was constantly buying my wife cards and flowers to apologize for my behavior, never once thinking about actually changing.

Another one of my "addicted personality" problems was my jokes. Most of them were (and, in fact, still are) very mean and "asshole-ish." I was always laughing *at* people, not *with* them. I told the jokes because they made *me* laugh. I didn't care how they might make other people feel.

It was now obvious to anyone who looked that I was in bad shape. Eventually, I realized it too. But my only strategy for change was to use one drug to help me get off another drug. It didn't work.

CHAPTER 25

Shaaren

It sounds far-fetched, but it often seems like I feel *everything*. It's not just observation, although I'm good at that, too. Sometimes, it's just sensing in the base of my ribs how somebody else is feeling. I've started to wonder if this trait is inherited because my daughter is the exact same way. I've come to believe that this is both a blessing and a curse. Being able to discern what others are feeling can be very useful and it often feels like a superpower. But such a skill has definitely put me at risk for becoming codependent. Sensing *what* somebody is feeling is very different from understanding *why* they feel that way. And yet, codependents often feel responsible for the "why." Or, at the very least, we think it's our job to "fix it".

I can't even say for certain when the addict-codependent relationship that Scott and I were in started to get really bad. It happened slowly, so it was hard to even see the changes. The thing about being the codependent in a relationship is that it's not just the alcoholic who lowers his standards. I lowered mine just as quickly as Scott lowered his. Things that I never thought I would put up with—his hangovers, his constant and unpredictable mood swings, our house reeking of booze—just became normal. And there were always more things…and then more. As I said before, there's no real tipping point in the process. Until, sometimes, there is.

I discovered Al-Anon meetings in late 2009 or early 2010. Scott's behavior had become so erratic and unpredictable and we were fighting a lot about his drinking. I knew I needed some kind of support. Being a stay-at-home momma with no babysitter for Ara, I only attended online meetings. Looking back, I think I probably chose those online meetings because I didn't want to tell a babysitter—or anyone else, for that matter—where I was going. Shame manifests itself in many ways. One of them is secrecy.

Even though these online meetings could never be the same as the regular, in-person ones, I don't know what I would have done without them. There's a quote that says "Alcoholism isn't a spectator sport. Eventually, the whole family gets to play" (Joyce Rebeta Burditt), and boy, was that true! I was so focused on him that I forgot about myself. Al-Anon mostly teaches you to focus on your own recovery. That's exactly what I needed at this point in my life—especially since I wasn't just responsible for myself now, but also for my daughter. The meetings really helped me learn to deal with the realities of living with an addict. Even though Scott's growing addiction while we were together happened slowly, coming to understand it—and my own reactions—was a steep learning curve.

I learned first that all addicts lie. It's not their fault, it's just what they do. And although addicts are certainly responsible for their own behavior, it is absolutely ridiculous to expect an addict *not* to lie. Yet, that's exactly what I did expect. I always believed Scott when he said he was going to limit his drinking or only drink beer or go to AA meetings or anything else. I believed him when he told me that the pills I had found in his work bag were from years ago. (I'm sure now that they were painkillers.) I believed him when he said he wanted to change. And when he said it wasn't as bad as it was.

Every time I discovered a new lie, it changed me. I'm not unique. Years of being lied to would change anyone. I used to be confident, I used to trust myself and my judgment, I used to be so strong. But being lied to all the time made me doubt everything. In every sentence that Scott uttered, there may have been two truths and two lies, but I never knew which was which.

I also never really knew the depth of Scott's addiction. When we first met, he had stopped smoking pot so easily. And he seemed to handle not drinking during my pregnancy so well. Of course, I didn't know at the time that he was hooked on pills. And that was why, despite him telling me that he had given up drinking again in early 2010 and that he was going to AA meetings, Scott kept getting worse and worse. At the same time he was bringing home "sobriety coins" from AA, he was also throwing back Oxycontin, Percoset, Vicodin and Tylenol with codeine. The combination of his lying, my own self-doubt, and the conflicting evidence I was always getting just fucked with my head.

All this made me ripe for manipulation. And Scott was a master at it. I never actually believed that his behavior was my fault. (Many addicts insist this is the case and many other people believe it too.) Even so, I certainly allowed any discussion (fight) that I had with Scott about his drinking to be twisted and turned so I couldn't tell which end was up. I'd start out telling him how much I didn't like his drinking. By the end of the conversation I'd be defending my *own* behavior and trying to prove that *I* wasn't being controlling.

One of *my* biggest problems in dealing with Scott (and one that I've learned many codependents struggle with) was my mouth. I always have a solution for everybody else's problems and I would much rather focus on their short-comings than my own. So many of our conversations started with me saying "You should..." or "You need to..." If Scott was actually following through on my demands, he'd get resentful. If he wasn't listening, he could still blame me for the stress I created by trying to control him.

CHAPTER 26

Shaaren

I spent most of the winter of 2010-11 putting ads in Craigslist and determining who would be interviewed by Chad or Scott, developing a new staff manual, and preparing for the reopening of Argo's completely renovated downstairs dining room, bar and kitchen. Scott and I were so grateful for all the help and support we had gotten since the fire that we were determined to repay our debts by taking our jobs even more seriously. We were going to change our rules and the way we managed Argo so we could focus on serving our customers better and improve our restaurant culture (how our team worked and behaved when we weren't present, how our team treated each other, how our team trained new people - essentially, "What is the Argonaut way?").

Because Scott and I had started out working at Argo as regular team members, it was hard for us to make the transition to being "management." Like any new managers, we made many rookie mistakes. There were paradigm shifts we had to work through—like no longer being friends with our staff. Emotionally, that was probably harder on us than it was on them. We had to start enforcing our rules, instead of just ignoring when staff broke them.

We were also changing our policies regarding the more "mundane", day-to-day operations. We were determined to improve our customer service after the fire. One of the ways to do that was to get our staff to treat Argo less like a party and more like work. First, we announced that there would be no more drinking during work and no more shift drinks. These practices were not unique to the Argonaut, it's just how many restaurants and bars operate. Allowing employees to drink while they work, or in the last hour, or offering one or two inexpensive drinks for free after their shift was over, is a common practice in most restaurants and bars. But, how could we be taken seriously as a workplace and in the community if everybody was under the influence? Are there any other industries where you're encouraged to be drunk or high while working?

To say no to this was pretty revolutionary, and it was also pretty unpopular.

We also said there would be no more hanging out at Argo after hours, and we created a Drug-Free Workplace Policy. Staff members were no longer allowed to come to work under the influence, or do drugs while at work.

Many of our employees did not like these changes, sending us texts and emails about how we "were ruining the Argonaut" but we told our staff that it was just part of the new Argo 2.0. "Get on board with the new rules or get off the ship."

I tried to read everything I could possibly read about restaurant management, team-building, and restaurant culture. It took me until the spring, but I eventually finished our new several-hundred-page Staff Manual, with an increased focus on the "why" of Argo. A part of me wonders, now, if I thought that these new laid out rules would be a way to control Scott's behavior, as well:

Defining Argonaut Culture – Why? What? How?

Why?

So why do we do what we do? What is our mission? What is the Argonaut's "why"? We do what we do because:

- *We want to serve our neighborhood and the greater H Street & Hill Community – not just now, but in the future. We want to grow and evolve together.*
- *We want to be a family to each other (and our customers). We believe it's important to treat every family member with respect.*
- *We want to demonstrate our belief that we don't have to do what everybody else does or has done before to be successful **and** that we are willing to learn from our successes.*
- *We want to demonstrate our belief that we are better because of our mistakes **and** that we are willing to learn from our mistakes.*

What?

What is our "Guest Service Objective"? What do we think our goal should be for every customer who walks through our door, eats, and leaves? What is the measure of our success?

- *We want everybody to leave feeling as if they are a part of our Argonaut Family. We want everybody to have had such an amazing experience that they simply cannot wait to return with their friends and family.*

How?

How are we going to get there? How do we need to change ourselves to ensure that what is special about the Argonaut will always be special for the community and for us?

- *We show up early.*
- *We work hard.*
- *We follow the rules.*

- *We have an amazing and infectious attitude. It is not the load that weighs us down, it's how we carry it.*
- *We are kind. Life is hard enough already – we do not need to make things harder for other people.*
- *We are cooperative, not competitive. We support each other.*
- *We are unafraid to ask for help when we need it. None of us can do this alone.*
- *We value collaborative thinking about challenges. When we have complaints, we offer solutions.*

Welcome to the Argonaut family.

Fixing the Argonaut and giving back what we had been given became an obsession for me. There wasn't a minute in the day that I didn't feel grateful for making it through the fire and its aftermath. In theory, there's nothing wrong with such immense gratitude, but I'm sure my version came off more zealot than Zen.

Right after we reopened in January 2011, I had become a master of detaching. I'd wake up in the middle of the night, Scott would be snoring loudly beside me, and the bedroom would reek of booze. At first I'd think, "I know I had wine at dinner, but this can't be me." Then, instead of lying awake worrying about what the more likely reality was—that Scott was drinking again and that he wasn't really sleeping, he was passed out—I would take a deep breath and try to go back to sleep. Thanks to Al-Anon, this was a complete change from my normal pattern of obsessing over every little thing, of staying awake for hours mulling over things that would only amp up my anxiety.

But no matter how hard I practiced detachment, there was no doubt that things were getting really bad with Scott again. He was short-tempered, always purposefully busy, and completely unavailable. To cope, I was working my Al-Anon program as hard as I could. Trying to detach from him, from my expectations, from the outcome. I wasn't very good at it.

Because I mostly went to online Al-Anon meetings, I didn't interact much with other addicts in recovery. I started a separate Twitter account for recovery and found a very supportive community via #xa [instead of identifying a specific program #AA, #NA, #SA, people use #xa to signify any recovery program]. I got to meet all sorts of people in recovery. It really helped solidify that *addiction* is the disease, *not* the substance. On top of the recovering drug addicts and alcoholics, I met sex addicts and partners of sex addicts, overeaters and people dealing with other eating disorders. And, of course, other Al-Anons. Because most of us were using anonymous handles, we could be even that much more open with and supportive of each other.

Plus, because I wasn't emotionally invested or codependently attached to them, I could hear what they were saying in a way that I just couldn't do with Scott. Their perspectives helped me with empathy, and they also just called me on my bullshit. A lot. What bullshit? When I'd forget and think I was in charge of his disease or recovery. When I'd complain about finding drugs—especially if I went looking for them. When I'd talk about how bad he was behaving instead of working on myself.

I'd create little ways to work my program [program speak for the changes we try to make in our behavior or reactions] by creating daily (Hourly! Minute-ly!) self-improvement projects for myself, just to get through the awful times. "Operation Thermostat" was one. Instead of being a thermometer, measuring the stress in the house, Scott's mood, or my own mood, I decided I would be a thermostat. No matter what he did, I was just going to stay calm. Sometimes, I found myself being a "Spiteful Thermostat", like, "I'm going to be happy and calm just to spite him" which is clearly the letter, but not the spirit.

Another one was "Operation Un-Prickle". His unpredictable behavior and anger made me resentful. I'd protectively close myself off when he was mean and be unable (and unwilling) to relax when he was having a good day. I was a cactus, regardless of how he was acting, so one of my projects was to not bristle when he was around. I can tell you right now that this project was rarely successful.

My detachment strategies didn't work too well when I woke up one morning around four o'clock and discovered that Scott still hadn't come home. I decided to check the feed from Argo's security cameras on my computer. Sure enough, there was Scott, taking shots and hanging out with patrons while bartending. For me, that image was devastating. And it was probably what gave Scott his new "permanent" residence on our living room couch.

I was also physically working really hard at Argo. I helped host on Friday and Saturday nights and managed and ran food during the day on Saturdays and Sundays with Ara in tow. I was exhausted.

Shaaren taking a break from food running and Scott taking
a break from cooking. Photo by Ara, March 19, 2011

I was filled with despair.

I felt lonely. I felt like I had no life except for the Argonaut and an addict—I felt trapped. I felt partner-less as Ara's only functioning parent. I felt so sad and angry that I couldn't trust my husband. Watching other families making vacation or future plans left me green with envy. I was so sad that our family was too sick to be able to plan for the next day, let alone a vacation or the future. It killed me when Ara would ask "Why can't Daddy make good decisions?".

Things had gotten so bad that I finally insisted he see a therapist. Scott was pissed at me for suggesting it, and annoyed that I even thought he had issues, but to my great surprise, he scheduled appointments *and* went to them!

I shouldn't have been surprised, though.

After just a session or two, he managed to score a prescription for Adderall. "No *wonder* he actually went to those appointments!" I was beyond nervous about this new prescription - I had heard and read things about how easy Adderall is to abuse.

* * * *

> *April 26, 2011—And, of course, he got a prescription for Adderall, so now I'm filled with anxiety. I need to relax, though, because his drugs of choice are always depressants, and not stimulants, so perhaps he won't have the desire to abuse.*
> *And, of course, there's nothing I can do about it.*
> *The doc left it up to him to mess with his own fucking dosage. And we all know who he is... But they are prescription happy and 2) seem to underestimate problems of addiction. So, she says to cut them in half if he's having problems. Which, to an addict, means also, double, or add more... As I've learned from experience. Especially since he's on the short term one right now. 4 hr increments. A recipe for self-medicating and abuse.*

* * * *

Some Twitter program friends talked me down from my ledge (because, as I had even said myself, there was nothing I could do about him using Adderall) and I relaxed a little. And, for a couple weeks, things were wonderful. I'd tell people that Adderall was miraculous and that I could finally see again the Scott from the beginning. The person who I had fallen in love with. I distinctly remember telling our new friends Maria and Patricia that Adderall had saved our marriage, had saved *us*.

Even when Chad warned me that Adderall is dangerous (especially for former and current cocaine users) I didn't want to listen. Talk about denial! I was so worried *before* Scott took the pills, yet, after he took them, it was still easier to think, "Well, that was the situation for *other people*. It certainly won't be like that for *us*."

But.

Chad was right.

* * * *

> *June 16, 2011—Sink at Argo broke again last night. Instead of calling a plumber, he stayed until 1 to fix it. So he could*

drink. Then stayed up until 4 because I think he manipulated his Adderall. I caught him messing with it a couple Fridays ago (when he'd been drinking), taking more than the regular dosage, so he doesn't get tired from the drinking.

Ara asks, "Where's daddy? Why isn't daddy home?" It's heartbreaking. I've started telling her that one of the ways he's sick is that he works too much...

* * * *

* * * *

June 26, 2011—The anger and split personalities are too much.

At any given moment, he will be:

Mean and nasty because he's overtired from not sleeping because of the medication.
Mean and nasty because he's overtired from not sleeping because he purposefully stayed out 'til all hours.
Mean and nasty because he's hungry from not eating.
Incompetent and mean because he drank.
Incompetent and high because he smoked pot.
High because he took a pill that he wasn't *prescribed.*
High because he took a pill he was *prescribed.*
Mean and nasty because he hasn't had tobacco.
Mean and nasty because he's hungover.
Amped up because he took too much Adderall.
Mean and nasty because he didn't take his Lexapro.
Mean and nasty because he didn't take his Chantix.
Mean because he didn't take his Adderall.
Buzzed because he took Clonazapam.
Not around because he ran away: "Maybe you'll see me in a couple days.".
Not around because he's hiding at work.
Not around because he's created a crisis at work.
Not around because he drank.
Not around because he smoked pot.
Not around because he took painkillers.

Not around because he took multiple doses of drugs he was prescribed.
Terrorizes us by saying things like: "Well, I might as well just smoke pot/drink/do whatever."
Terrorizes us by leaving and not saying where he's going or when he's coming back.
Terrorize me by throwing things at me, slamming doors, screaming, swearing.

Sometimes, he apologizes and acts honestly sad about the way he has behaved.
But that always goes quickly and is replaced by all of the above.

* * * *

In Al-Anon, there's no rule book about having "the strength to stay, or the strength to go." I had told myself that when it was time to leave, I'd know. For a long time, I did have the strength to stay. And then one day I didn't. I had hit my own bottom.

I bought two plane tickets for Ara and me to go stay with my parents. A few days later, on June 30, 2011, after things had been so awful for so many months, I took our three-year-old daughter and walked out of our house. Scott drove us to BWI airport and I will never forget it. He pulled up to the curb and got our stuff out of the car. We said goodbye, both of us with tears in our eyes, and Ara and I headed to check-in. This was such a pivotal moment, maybe even more so than buying the tickets. Not only was I leaving, but...he was letting me.

He let us go.

CHAPTER 27

Scott

Everyone's bottom is different.

My wife had just taken our daughter to her parents' house to escape my destruction. It was no surprise when Shaaren left. She had warned me. *She* was tired of my behavior and *I* was convinced she was the problem. We were at an impasse. Why did she have to be so controlling? Why wasn't I allowed to be with *my* daughter? My anger and frustration with the whole situation made me want to get away, too. I decided to take a trip of my own—in the other direction. I drove down to my old stomping grounds in Virginia Beach to "clear my head"—meaning, of course, to get fucked up!

I booked a hotel room at the Virginia Beach Resort and Conference Center. The Resort had been my go-to place to stay whenever I returned to Virginia Beach for a visit. It was centrally located on Chesapeake Beach and a short drive to the Virginia Beach oceanfront. Most of my friends from my teenage years still lived in the area. Growing up, we spent many nights sneaking into the Resort's pool or using its parking lot when we went to the beach. I planned on staying for a couple of days before heading back to D.C. to check on things at the Argonaut.

I had decided that my trip down to Virginia Beach would be my last hurrah. I was going to enjoy myself, get fucked up, and then head up to see Shaaren and Ara. While I was out at a bar near the hotel, Shaaren called my cell phone. I chose to ignore her call and continued hanging out with some of my old friends. I eventually returned her call the next morning.

I returned to D.C. for a few nights to check on Argo and did what everyone would have done when faced with a life of misery—I partied and went bar hopping. I ended up bringing a couple of people back to our house and we sat out back drinking until early morning. The next day I felt like shit. I woke up really late, cleaned up the house, and got on the road.

Shaaren had made it clear when she called me in Virginia Beach that she wouldn't let me come up to her parents' house until she believed I was a changed man. Like always, I told her I had shaped up and was ready to see my family again. Heading up to Massachusetts, I still thought I could make our life together work. At least I wanted to try. I had promised her I was done with the drinking, but she still didn't know the extent of my painkiller use. And I was kind of hoping she never would, as I was seriously considering giving them up.

I made it as far as New Jersey, before I started nodding off behind the wheel. I decided I better find a hotel room for the night. I called Shaaren and told her there had been an accident and traffic was really backed up. After checking into a hotel, I went out and had dinner. I was so sick from the night before, I could only drink one beer. I went back to the hotel and fell asleep.

I had decided that I could maybe live with just my Klonopin and Adderall—typical me, using one drug to get off another. As a result, I spent the week at Shaaren's parents' house sick and crazed.

Scott helping Ara learn to skateboard, July 3, 2011

I was sweating, throwing up, and always about to cry. To anyone with eyes, I was an emotional mess. But I didn't tell anybody what was really wrong with me—I was detoxing from my painkillers while still upping my dosages of Klonopin and Adderall. Shaaren had no idea what was wrong with me and suggested I call my sponsor. Which, to her (and my!) surprise, I did.

For some reason, a week later, Shaaren and I agreed that we would go back home as a family.

CHAPTER 28

Shaaren

Finally, after Ara and I left D.C. to stay with my parents, Scott was alone with his disease. And I was alone with mine.

It wasn't until I had left Scott that I started to see my own enabling behaviors. And I was a great enabler! Once I was away from him, I realized that I never let him miss a business meeting or appointment. He could be passed out or completely hung over and I'd diligently get him up and ready to go. Maybe he would have hit his bottom a lot quicker if he had missed some of those meetings with his business partner, Joe.

Another enabling behavior was that I rarely spoke honestly about Scott's behavior to anyone except at online Al-Anon meetings. I took his shame and I made it mine.

Instead of ignoring Scott's temper and walking out of the room when he got crazy, I would jump right in and get dragged down with him. By engaging, I allowed him to convince himself that *I* was the problem. As long as he could blame me, he never had to blame his addiction.

I'd forget that he had a disease and I'd be constantly disappointed by my own expectations. I'd believe his words instead of looking at his actions. And then I'd get resentful and be angry. Not that any of it was my fault, but I really offered no incentive for him to change his behavior.

I'd pour his alcohol down the drain and try to control his drinking in other ways. I'd ask him constantly if he was high, if he was drunk, if he had used. I'd go through his pockets and check his bag. I'd smell his breath. I'd search the car. I forced him to take drug tests and shamed him constantly. While I didn't create the problem, I certainly exacerbated the situation and made it impossible for him to be honest with me. I insisted that he go to AA meetings and find a sponsor. I was always so mad at him for behaving poorly that I never gave him presents. Like, ever. And I withdrew my love.

It might sound justified, no? Addicts can do truly horrible and awful things, and Scott certainly was absolutely no exception. But, these were *my* own horrible behaviors, not his.

And, instead of detaching or leaving, I stayed and continued my codependent relationship. Our addicts are hooked on substances, and we are addicted to our addicts.

Perhaps if I hadn't tried so hard to control and help…perhaps if there had been more times when he didn't make it home to me and Ara because he had passed out somewhere…perhaps he would have realized the effects of his drinking and drugging earlier…perhaps he would have stopped.

But he didn't. And maybe that was because I was more than willing to take on the burden of his addiction.

Through Al-Anon, I began to understand that these were all normal behaviors and reactions to living with such insanity. We try to control little parts of the chaos to make our lives feel less chaotic. These behaviors were part of *my disease*, which was forgetting that, along with the addict, I, too, was powerless over his alcohol and drugs.

Even if I had followed the Al-Anon way "perfectly," there was no guarantee that Scott would have ever hit his bottom. I've learned that only the luckiest of addicts hit bottom, recognize it, and decide they've had enough.

A little over two weeks after reaching my bottom, he reached his, too. What a blessing!

Ara and I came back home with Scott to empty promises. I'm still not sure why I agreed to go back with him, and I've spent a lot of time thinking about it. I know I felt that staying with my parents was an imposition. Ara and I had already been there for two weeks. I also felt like I was neglecting the work I was responsible for at Argo. And I guess Ara and I had missed him. Plus, let's not forget DENIAL.

Predictably, less than two hours after we got back home, Scott started drinking again.

The three of us had walked over to Argo and Ara and I sat down at our table. Scott went to put our food orders in behind the bar. When I turned around and looked back, I saw him chugging a beer. I suggested that he go to an AA meeting or at least call his sponsor. Then I took Ara home, tucked her in, and crawled into bed myself. Go, Team Detachment!

I woke up around eleven that night and Scott still wasn't home. I started to get worried. I still had no idea that he had this whole other sneaking-out-of-the-house life. That it was *normal* for him to leave the house after I had gone to sleep. My hard-won detachment went right out the window. I called his cell phone over and over, but got no answer. Frantic, I opened up the computer and checked the feed from Argo's security cameras.

There he was, sitting at a table eating with two of our employees. My sanity quickly departed. I called and called the Argonaut's phone and watched as Scott and our employees just sat there letting the phone ring. I felt stupid, betrayed, and absolutely bat-shit crazy.

Eventually, Scott answered the phone and I convinced him to come home. He walked in about an hour later (from two blocks away). Right away he said he was going to an AA meeting and left again. I thought at the time that AA had meetings twenty-four hours a day. It turned out they didn't. I remember feeling so scared and so angry, so hurt and *so done* with all this.

Scott finally walked back in around five o'clock that morning. Like a true codependent, I went downstairs to tell him what I thought of him. He sat down on the couch and confessed not only to drinking again, but to having a five-pills-a-day painkiller habit for the last five years.

I called him an asshole, told it was time for inpatient treatment, and walked back upstairs.

Finding out the truth was devastating. But strangely, I didn't feel so crazy anymore. All that lying, all those mixed messages, all that time where nothing was getting better? It was finally explained. The truth, while hard to hear, had set me free.

An hour later, I heard Scott talking on the phone with our health insurance company. He was asking about treatment centers.

And for the first time, I felt hope.

CHAPTER 29

Shaaren

Scott entered treatment on July 12, 2011.

The day he left, I felt both panicked and calm. And, for the first time, I felt somewhat compassionate because I could see how broken he was. After he left, though, that quickly changed back into anger. I mean, I was angry. Like, Stab-Him-With-A-Fork ANGRY. I felt that our entire relationship had been a lie because he was high the whole time. High when we got married. And when our daughter was born. Every time we drove somewhere. Every vacation. Every *intimate* moment. How could he possibly know if he even liked me, much less *loved* me?

And even scarier, how did I know if I even liked *him*? Who was he, really?

Scott had managed to spend most of his life skirting the consequences of his actions. That didn't change after he left. While he was in his first full day of treatment, I was sitting in our living room with Ara, my neighbor Nancy, and her kids. I heard some noise outside and when I looked out the window, our car was getting booted. It turned out that Scott had neglected to pay thousands of dollars worth of parking and speeding tickets.

Addiction: the gift that keeps on giving!

Shortly after Scott entered inpatient treatment in Florida, I made a lot of calls trying to find a therapist in our neighborhood who would accept our health insurance. I finally found a woman who fit the criteria and I started seeing her while Scott was away. Therapy proved extremely useful in helping me keep the focus on myself—not an easy task given how closely Scott and I lived our lives.

From the beginning, the life we had together was quite different from that of many, perhaps even most, couples. Scott and I had always worked together. When things started to get bad for us as a couple, they were also getting bad for him—and us—at work. Scott became more and more irrational and unpredictable. He would flip out about the most random and stupid things. One time, he forced Chad to tell anybody he caught using one of his pens that he'd fire them. He set a horrible example as a boss. And the example he set as a father and husband, not only because he never really wanted to be with us, but also because of his temper and impatience, wasn't any better. The destruction and turmoil that an addict leaves in his path is far-reaching, so, along with his family, several years' worth of Argo employees were also affected by Scott's addiction and our dysfunction.

The business itself was an interesting predicament while Scott was in treatment. I had spent the months since our January reopening trying to rally our staff around the Argonaut and make it a better place. I was busy trying to bail out the water and save the ship, not knowing that, the whole time, Scott was making the holes in our sinking boat even *bigger*. Now I felt embarrassed and humiliated that *everybody* at work had known he was sneaking back to Argo at night and drinking again. I seemed to be the only one who didn't have a clue.

Once Scott entered treatment, I promised myself that I would do everything I could do to not only to keep Argo going, but also to keep myself from falling apart. Even though I didn't want to, I knew that Ara and I had to go there every night for dinner as we always had. I would have preferred anything to this, but it was the right thing to do and I did it. This wasn't the same as me rallying after the fire. This time, panic and adrenaline had been replaced by resolve and depression. But If I failed, if I didn't go, I knew that the Argonaut could be lost to us. All the positive changes we were making would disappear and we'd have to start over. Changing a restaurant's internal culture is possible, but it's time-consuming. I knew staff would probably be breaking rules left and right when I wasn't there, but at least through the dinner rush, everything would be fine. Argo, like my house, was much calmer without Scott. But it was awful, too. I was overwhelmed with loneliness. Going to the Argonaut each night, having to be in public, seeing people whose lives weren't being wrecked by addiction, only amplified my feelings. Plus, I had no peer-level friends at Argo. It was so isolating.

Scott didn't want our staff to know where he really was. He said I should tell everyone that he was off surfing. And mostly, I listened to him. While I believe that honesty is always good, it can sometimes put too much pressure on people in early recovery. Since relapse is so common, it can add another level of shame where one certainly isn't needed. And, as part of our new rules, I wasn't really friends with any of the staff. I'm not sure it was the right decision, but at the time, we felt nothing good could have come from them officially knowing the real reason for Scott's absence at this point. I'm sure they all just thought I had finally kicked him out.

I was very strategic in choosing the few people I did tell. Our kitchen manager, Noris, for instance, because she had known Scott for years. Joe, Cheryl (Joe's office manager) because they needed to know. And because I also thought I would need their support to get Scott to continue treatment once he returned to D.C. Some people were genuinely surprised when I told them the truth. Some people thought I was overreacting or exaggerating, which was *extremely* frustrating. I wanted to scream! It wasn't like *I* checked him into rehab—he went himself! Predictably, I could tell that others weren't surprised. They knew what the situation was. Scott hadn't tried to hide his life from them. Just from me.

My family knew and Scott had told his father before he left. And my close friends knew. Scott had also told the young woman who was his office assistant, and our bartender, Ryan, the truth. Ryan was the only person at work with whom I could talk to about the real situation.

In some ways, Scott being in treatment made my life so much easier. I didn't have to constantly pick up the slack when I had thought I could count on him. I didn't have to deal with his tantrums and unpredictability. Compared to what it had been, our house seemed like an oasis.

Ara was amazing and strong while Scott was away. She had complete faith that her Daddy would be coming back. She knew that her Daddy loved her very much. She also knew that she could always count on me. Scott and I had always tried to be open with her about his illness. We didn't talk specifically about drugs or drinking because she was far too young.

But when Scott left for treatment, I did use very simple, but true words to explain why her father was away. "Daddy is sick in his brain and needs to go to special, special doctors," I told her. Most of the time she didn't seem to mind that he was gone. After all, she didn't see him that much when he was around.

It was a very hard time. And it wasn't just being a single parent. I had been playing that role for months. It wasn't just running a business by myself. And even though there were nights when Ara and I would fall asleep in my bed with me holding her in my arms and both of us crying, it wasn't that, either.

The hardest thing was simply seeing and being around normal, happy families.

In treatment Scott was turning out to be a tough nut to crack. His counselor called me a couple of times at home and told me that Scott was one of the most challenging patients they ever had. This was awful news, but it also made me feel less crazy. If trained professionals were at their wits' end, I never stood a chance!

Scott's counselor was happy to hear that I was a seasoned Al-Anon member and that I had no intention of encouraging Scott to leave treatment. Apparently, many codependents do. He told me he was trying to get a special pass for Scott to use the telephone several days earlier than the rules allowed. He wanted to use it as leverage to force Scott to stay in treatment. The counselor assured me that he'd call me during Scott's next session if it was going badly. Thankfully, he never called again, but just talking to him those two times left me terrified. His words only reinforced how high the stakes were. This was it. This was Scott's only chance, *our* only chance as a family. And it might not work.

I will never forget those two phone calls.

While Scott was in treatment, I sent him some photos of Ara and me. But I never wrote him any letters. I was still struggling to process so many things. I couldn't get outside of my own perception of what was happening. And, quite honestly, I had no idea what to say to him.

CHAPTER 30

❦

Scott

This is addiction. I actually believed these were two rational choices of equal value - my wife and daughter or drugs and alcohol. That's how sick I was.

I found myself walking up and down H Street all cracked out until about four in the morning. When I finally went home, I saw—for the first time, really—the look of hurt in my wife's eyes.

It still haunts me. That was what it took. I knew I had to choose.

This was the first time in my life that I chose my family over drugs and alcohol.

Coming home after that blur of a night on H Street, I finally saw my life as the mess it was. I was destroying everyone and everything in my path. I had absolutely no skills to deal with any kind of emotions—my own or other peoples'. I was alone. And I was scared.

I wish I could say it was easy, but it was not. Deciding to go into treatment was the hardest thing I have ever done in my life. But I finally admitted to myself that I had a problem and that my life was no longer manageable. By choosing to get myself into treatment, I was also admitting to everyone in my world and beyond that I was an addict.

I set about finding a treatment center that had space available, would accept my health insurance, and met my "vacation" requirements. Since the Four Seasons in Maui was not an option, I settled for a stay in Palm Beach, Florida. After some internet searches and phone calls, I had found a treatment center called Behavioral Health of the Palm Beaches that would take me right away. BHOPB had three different facilities—depending on your ability (or your insurance company's willingness) to pay. If money wasn't an issue, you could get clean at the "seaside residences" in West Palm Beach. Down the ladder a few rungs were the single-gender residences. At the low end (mine) was something called "The Cottages" in Palm Beach. That sounded fine to me. They signed me up over the phone and told me what I should and could bring—insurance card, prescription card, all meds (in original bottles), some money, cigarettes, a personal CD or MP3 player (without an internet connection), casual clothing, a bathing suit and sunscreen. And what I could not bring—no weapons, cell phones, computers, musical instruments, stereo equipment, provocative clothing, playing cards, valuables, or clothing or other items promoting sex, drugs, or alcohol.

Being the stubborn and selfish addict I was, I decided I would *drive* down to Florida. I thought the drive would help me "clear my head" a bit before starting my vacation. It took some doing, but Shaaren, my therapist, and my dad finally convinced me it would not be a wise move to drive. Reluctantly, I booked a ticket on the next available flight that day out of BWI and packed my bag. So much for my "one last hurrah" road trip. I stopped by the Argonaut and broke down as I told Ryan, our bartender, what was happening. The rest of the morning I ran errands and tried to figure out ways to make it as easy as possible for Shaaren, Ryan and the office manager to run the Argonaut while I was away.

Then I went home to say goodbye to Ara and Shaaren. Although she wasn't seething with anger towards me, it wasn't much of a goodbye. I didn't know what Shaaren was thinking, but I was pretty sure our marriage was about over. Saying goodbye to Ara broke my heart. I was so ashamed. What had I done? I was glad I was heading somewhere far enough away so I could hide. Our office manager drove me to Union Station where I caught a train to the airport.

I arrived at the Palm Beach airport around eleven o'clock that night and there was a van waiting for me. The driver said we had to wait for one more person. My nerves were shot. And I was having serious doubts about my decision to do this thing. It was about a twenty-minute drive to the detox facility in Lake Worth. I didn't say a word during the trip, just stared out the window. I hated myself and all I wanted to do was go to sleep and forget about everything.

Soon enough, we reached what looked like some kind of compound surrounded by a tall fence with a white gate that opened and closed to let cars in and out. Welcome to detox! The facility consisted of a commons area and two houses—one for male addicts and one for female addicts. Each house had four rooms and each room held two people. My fellow passenger and I were escorted to an intake area where we were given drug and Breathalyzer tests. Since I had a beer at the airport, I was surprised when I blew .00 on the Breathalyzer. My bag and I were both searched and I was asked all sorts of questions about what drugs I had used, and when, and what I was currently on. All my drugs, including my prescription meds, were taken away.

"What do you mean you're taking my Adderall and Klonopin?" I yelled. "A licensed doctor gave them to me! They are mine!" I could understand them taking away my non-prescription painkillers, but the other ones had been prescribed for me! My arguments weren't very persuasive. I was told that if I needed drugs, they had doctors who could prescribe them. I think that was when it really hit me what kind of place this was.

I was a sad sight when I entered treatment that night. At five feet, nine inches tall, I weighed 140 pounds. I hadn't shaved my head for a few weeks and I looked like a skinny junkie—which, of course, I was. But, typically, as I looked around at everyone else in the detox area, I told myself, "They are much worse than you are." Each person was in a different stage of detoxing off of different drugs. It looked like a clip from Night of the Living Dead.

I didn't want to be in this detox area and I was trying as hard as I could to talk my way out and into the "normal" program. For once, I talked and no one listened. I was stuck. Then the staff asked me about taking some meds to help me get through the detox process. I figured I had detoxed on my own at Shaaren's parents' house and I could do it again. I told "my keepers" I didn't need any meds now. What a mistake that was! Unlike me, everyone else was chilled out. Whatever they were handing out had these people really *fucked up*! I mean, they *couldn't even talk*. I wanted what *they* were having! But I had told them I didn't need meds to detox.

Detox was the beginning of having no control over anything. We had a few structured group classes and a lot of down time just waiting, talking, and trying to sleep. I was so tired but I couldn't fall asleep. For almost twenty years, downers had helped me sleep. Now my body was confused. It had no idea how to sleep on its own. We had speakers come in and talk to us about AA and NA and when and how they got sober. One of the speakers gave me my first introduction to meditation. At first I really didn't understand it. All I knew was that it helped slow my mind down. A nifty little trick, I thought to myself. I think I like this meditation stuff.

After several days in detox, I joined several other patients who were judged ready to begin inpatient treatment at The Cottages. We piled into a van and off we went. We stopped at what our driver said was the "CADS" (Center for Alcohol and Drug Studies) building, an unassuming brick structure that looked like it might house a couple of businesses. We drove around the back and there was another gate to go through. Once inside the place, my mouth dropped. What had I gotten myself into? I was older than everyone here by a good ten or fifteen years. Most of the kids hanging around weren't even old enough to drink legally! Fortunately, it was a short visit. We were just dropping off a couple of the underage kids. The driver told us we had just been to the "Kiddie CADS" building and not the one for adults. Thank God! Most of the older heads in my group were raging alcoholics and I fit right in.

Finally, we reached The Cottages. They were a group of duplexes on a dead end road. Like the other facilities, a locked gate separated us from the real world. The first cottage on the right was the administration building where the counselors hung out. The whole complex had six identical duplexes. Each duplex had two, two-bedroom apartments, each with a nice kitchen and living space. Each apartment housed four people of the same sex, but different ages. The staff tried to make sure there was at least one adult in the group. I was the only person in my apartment over thirty. My three roommates were between eighteen and twenty-five. Every morning a counselor came in and checked to make sure our beds were made, the dishes had been done, and the place was clean.

Although I can laugh now about my experience in treatment, it didn't seem at all funny at the time. My therapist was probably in his late twenties. He was very skilled and pulled no punches. I was angry and he *really* knew how to push my buttons. I had a few one-on-one sessions with him, but normally we had small group meetings. We all sat in a circle and talked about feelings and shit. I was always combative and quick with my responses, plus I complained about *everything*. My therapist soon crowned me "King Baby." And not long after that, and because I was so difficult, he made me sit in the middle of the room and listen to everyone say what they didn't like about me. I was not allowed to say anything. I just had to sit and listen. During the whole time I sat there, my anger grew and my resentment toward my therapist grew. The worst part was—I had nothing to numb it with.

Being newly sober for the first time, I needed to control everything. But as anyone who has gone through this knows, in treatment you have no control over anything. I didn't like that and I wanted out! What made me really mad at first was that I couldn't even use the phone. I owned a bar, damn it, and I *needed* to have contact with the outside world. I was special!

I knew exactly how many days my insurance would pay for. One of the first things I did was put an end date on my treatment, originally trying to leave on that first Saturday. I also tried to use every bit of information I was getting about myself in therapy and turn it against my therapist. I unleashed response after response trying to reverse the roles and blame him. It was a technique I had mastered to hide my addiction from my wife. I had become the king of shifting focus and blame, always managing to reverse everything to put the blame on Shaaren. It worked great on her, but this was a less effective tactic against my therapist, who knew exactly what I was doing. And really, how was someone I had *just* met really responsible for anything in my life?

It took me about a week to calm down enough so that I wasn't yelling during every therapy session. I had no clue what bad shape I was in. I was so lost and I had convinced myself that all of my lies were the truth. I had bottled up so much, kept so much inside for so long, and hadn't let anyone get close. No one knew who I really was—not my wife, not my friends, and especially not me.

By the end of that first week, I had made friends with a few other patients. There was quite a bit of down time when we just sat around, watched the lizards, and talked a lot of shit. We made fun of everyone and everything—whatever made us feel better about ourselves. Because we all lived together in The Cottages, we had a great time making fun of our counselors and the younger "kids." I couldn't believe some of the creative ways they had figured out to get high. Snorting and shooting up Oxycontin or other painkillers? Holy Shit! Mixing painkillers and cocaine was another big thing. Just thinking about some of that shit made me a little sick, and that was saying something! And their new slang...I was always wondering, "What the fuck does *that* mean?"

Eventually, the days began to settle into a kind of routine. A weird routine, but still. We would wake up at six-thirty, make breakfast and pack a lunch. At eight the bus would leave to take us to either the adolescent or the adult CADS counseling center. We would stay at the center until four o'clock with an hour break in the middle of the day for lunch. Each hour, a different group meeting was scheduled. Some days, it seemed like all we did was sit forever just listening to some person babble away. For a change, one hour might be an AA movie, followed by a group discussion. Sometimes we would break into same-sex groups and talk some more. Every week was the same. Same schedule, same instructors talking about the same fucking thing, over and over and over like a broken record.

For me, at least at first, there was really only one bright spot in this daily routine. Every day, we had a guided group meditation. We were given instructions on how to meditate and what the benefits were. I had always had a problem with just sitting around and doing nothing. As a kid with ADHD, I could never sit still. And as an adult and an addict, I always had to be out doing something. I was actually terrified of simply sitting with myself. The boredom that "just sitting" brought on was my second biggest trigger for substance use, right behind opening my eyes in the morning.

In these guided meditation group meetings, someone talked you through the meditation process, told you how to breathe, helped you follow your breath and showed you how to bring your mind back to your breath when it wandered away. It was a very good introduction for the beginning meditator's untrained mind. It forced me to sit with myself and look at myself. That usually didn't go very well. I cried a lot. I had so many pent-up emotions that I had never even acknowledged, much less learned how to deal with. In fact, I realized I had no skills to deal with much of anything. My life was fucked!

And now that some time had passed and I finally had phone privileges, I couldn't even have a productive conversation with my wife.

Every time I called Shaaren, she and I would get into a screaming match. I couldn't understand why she was always so pissed at me. After all, I had done the right thing, hadn't I? By the end of every phone call I was either cussing or crying. I tried to grasp the reason I was being treated this way. I had told my fellow "recoverers" and counselors that my wife loved me and that we were happy. But then we'd have these terrible phone conversations. I truly could not put it together.

I guess, in my own mind, I thought that our relationship was still positive. Shaaren had stayed with me, after all. I felt that everything should be forgiven because I had entered treatment. I had been so self-absorbed for so long. I had no clue about the pain I had caused. I didn't understand that it wasn't just about my *own* self-destruction. I had destroyed my family as well. I was incapable of empathy. Put myself in someone else's shoes? Why the hell would I do that? My shoes were just fine, thank you.

Hard as it was, I really started to get into the meditation thing. The more I learned about it and struggled to just sit, the more it spoke to me. At some point, it began to have a powerful calming effect that I had never experienced before. I had been going to AA meetings for years and they never did a thing for me. I had still ended up in rehab. Now I started craving meditation.

For once, I had no outside stress. I had nothing to do but work on myself, either alone or in a group. For the first time ever, I was learning how to be with myself and be comfortable with that. I was learning about myself and my life. Every once in a while, I would smile.

After our all-day group meetings ended at four o'clock, we had the option of going back to The Cottages or to the gym. I went to the gym a few times and I even started jogging around the compound in the mornings. Quite a change for a person who bragged about never exercising. But the truth was, now that I was sober, I would try anything that might help me sleep. Around five o'clock, our house would start making dinner. We were given a food allowance and driven to the local Winn Dixie once a week to buy what we needed. Most evenings, I would cook something for my group on the grill, which I didn't mind at all. Around seven o'clock, we either had an AA meeting at The Cottages, or we got in the van and went out somewhere to a meeting.

One Tuesday night while we were riding in the van to that night's meeting, someone told me it was being held at a church. I hated churches—almost as much as I hated hospitals. The last time I had stepped foot in a church was for my mother's funeral. No one was ever going to get me inside a church again!

By the time the van reached the church, the hair on my arms was standing on end. The King Baby simply refused to go in. I yelled and cussed and wouldn't leave the van. I had convinced myself that church was evil. I was sure I would burst into flames if I walked into this damn place. Besides my mother's funeral, I hadn't been to church since I was a teenager. I hated it then, and they certainly didn't like me. Of course, that was because I would get high as a kite before I went to the youth group meetings and the coordinator could see right through me and was not amused. King Baby, indeed.

The counselors didn't know what to do. Finally, some of my peers persuaded me to enter the church and go to the room where the AA meeting was being held. I made sure everyone knew that I was only going in because of my friends.

I sat down and started talking to a man who said he was a regular at the meeting. It soon came out that I was from D.C. and owned a bar on Capitol Hill called the Argonaut. His response was, "*The Argonaut?* I know the Argonaut! I *love* the Argonaut!" There I was at an AA meeting in a *fucking church* in Palm Beach, Florida, and the one person I found to talk to not only knew the Argonaut, but loved it!

Maybe church wasn't so bad after all.

Weekends were different. On Saturdays there were no scheduled activities except a nightly AA meeting. During the day, we had the option of staying at the compound or going to the beach. Those weekly trips to the beach were wonderful therapy—much better than any trips to AA meetings or anywhere else. But what a sight we must have been. A bunch of people in rehab rolling up to the public beach in a big van. We all carried white towels and there was a perimeter we had to stay within. Nothing says treatment like a boundary line and a white towel. Still, it was nice to be on a beach. It was one of the few places where I always felt comfortable.

On Sundays, most people went to church. Except me. I preferred to continue my group work at the smaller, Sunday group meetings. Little did I realize at the time that my refusal to attend church on one particular Sunday would change my whole way of thinking and would help pave the way to a completely new approach to life. At the group meeting that Sunday, I watched a documentary about a guy named Noah Levine called "Meditate and Destroy."[iii] Levine was a California kid who started down a path of destruction at a very early age. In and out of juvenile detention, he eventually found himself on the street with a serious drug and alcohol problem. He ended up in a padded cell and started using meditation as a way to calm his brain and quiet his thoughts. That practice changed the direction of his life.

I could really connect with Noah Levine's life story. I liked the guided meditation sessions I had already been to. In fact, other than trips to the beach, they were about the only things I did like about inpatient treatment. Levine's experience confirmed for me that this was something worth sticking with.

As the end of my stay in rehab got closer, I decided the new me needed a new look. I had already shaved the fuzz on the top of my head and the rug that had grown on my neck. Now I shaved my beard and decided to go with a soul patch instead. I had managed to get a good tan. And in the twenty-one days I was there, I gained twenty-five pounds. I was ready to leave this place at a respectable 165 pounds. Who knew that not doing drugs *and* eating a real breakfast, lunch, and dinner could do that?

I'm pretty sure all the counselors expected to see me back in treatment very soon. Maybe they thought the second time around they would be able to get through to me. Knowing they felt that way, I was determined to do everything in my power to prove them wrong. That was just me being who I had always been. Stubborn. About everything.

But just in case. . . I still had those few extra days of insurance coverage. I decided that if I needed a break from D.C., I could always return for a few more days of R and R at The Cottages.

CHAPTER 31

Shaaren

While Scott was going through inpatient treatment in Florida, he could only use the phone every second or third day. He wrote a couple letters to me and Ara that were both wonderful and heartbreaking. It was wonderful to read how much he loved us.

* * * *

July 16, 2011
Dear Ara-Bug,

Daddy is so sorry about his selfish behavior. I love and miss you so very much. I hope you can one day understand, and that you know when you're older I will be able to explain the sickness that Daddy has.

I can't wait to see you so we can go skateboarding, ride bikes and be together.

They have lots of lizards here and the weather is really hot!

I love you my little Ara-Bug.
Love,
Daddy

* * * *

But even though he kept insisting he was sorry, I had heard that all before.

* * * *

July 16, 2011
Dear Shaaren,

My love. I am so very sorry for all of this. I love you so very much. The feelings of shame and abandonment I have right now are tearing me apart. I can't believe I have made it come to this. It's Saturday evening. I'm stuck in a limbo situation as the cottages are full and I'm in a house in a different area being shuffled back and forth. I still have not been allowed to use a phone and at this point I probably would be spending the whole time talking to you crying. My selfishness has become so apparent to me now. Please forgive me. You have been right the whole time and trying to fix a drug problem with another drug being prescribed really fucked me up. I owe you so much. You have taken it all on and are such a strong person. I admire and love you so much. I have been so scared to tell you the truth, and scared to admit to myself how truly awful I have been. To think about the damage I have caused. Please forgive me. I miss you so much and want to come home and see you!

I love you!

I'm ready to put everything in the past and move forward with you in love and happiness.

* * * *

It seemed that he thought deciding to get inpatient treatment was all he needed to do and, after that, his work was done. Call it optimism or naiveté on his part. But for me, it was just so depressing and scary to read.

Even though I was supposed to be working on myself while Scott was away, I was still very good at telling him how he should be working on his own program. Despite being separated by so many states for a number of weeks, we would slip back into our old patterns of dysfunction whenever we talked on the phone. In fact, nearly every phone conversation we had ended in a fight. I couldn't see past my own anger, I couldn't hear how broken he was or the hurt in his voice, and I couldn't tell how much work he was doing.

Plus, and let's not forget this part, he was insane.

I wrote to my friend Maya on July 23, 2011 that he says things like:

* * * *

"I know I can't control you and I have to make it up to you and build back all the trust. But then, you have to respect my decision to leave because the only thing I can control is myself."

"You want me to stay here wasting time getting a sunburn and bullshitting? You'd prefer me to smoke two packs a day and a gallon of coffee?!"

And then all the other stuff about needing to leave and it's terrible and how they treat him so badly and he just needs to leave.

* * * *

For some reason, he also convinced himself that his first priority should be to go to Missouri and see his deceased mother.

* * * *

Jul 25, 2011, 6:11am via Web (Twitter)
AH trying to tell me that if I were nicer/more supportive that he'd stay [in treatment], but "I should know" that he'll do opposite of what I want. 3Cs. [program speak for I did not cause, I can't control, I can't cure this disease]

Jul 25, 2011, 7:14am via Web (Twitter)
Yes! And, he likes to assert aggressively "I'M AT PEACE WITH MYSELF!". It's not very convincing... ;)

* * * *

Scott's therapist in DC and his inpatient counselor in Florida decided that, because our insurance was about to run out, Scott should come home after three weeks and use the remaining insurance coverage for outpatient treatment in D.C. I wasn't ready for him to come home, but I knew that outpatient was the right next step. Scott had a different plan— including saving up some insurance coverage to fly back down to Florida for a "break." He was *not* planning to continue treatment at an outpatient facility when he got back home. Knowing this, my own plan was to enlist Joe and Cheryl to help me convince him to continue treatment.

* * * *

July 26, 2011

> *I know this is a difficult subject...*
>
> *I have spoken with Scott several times and even though he's sober for the first time (probably since he was 14), his illness is in full effect. He is convinced that he has nothing else to learn, that he's virtually "cured" and is still blaming everybody else for his behavior. This is typical of all addicts, don't worry!*
>
> *Joe, I talked with Cheryl about his actual addiction yesterday. I learned the night before he checked himself in that he's been addicted to painkillers for 5 years (Vicodin, Percoset, OxyContin, Hydrocodone, Tylenol with Codeine). He confessed to me 5 pills/ day for 5 years, which I'm sure actually translates to something like 10 pills/day for 10 years. He's been drinking more frequently, too. I found out after he left that he was sneaking back to Argo almost every night to enjoy his pills/drink. He also abused his prescribed Adderall (ADHD) and Clonazepam (to combat the Adderall), as well as the Lexapro (anti-depressant) and Chantix (anti-tobacco). As you can imagine, this is all very dangerous.*
>
> *I emailed with Scott's therapist (in DC) yesterday and she believes that Kolmac's intensive outpatient program is the best place for Scott for when he decides to come home which will probably be August 1st, (if not sooner, since our insurance coverage only covers 20 days in treatment).*
>
> *I also believe it's his only shot at a chance at recovery. His denial runs deep, he's been using longer than most, and painkiller addiction is extremely hard to deal with, so they have their work cut out for them. Kolmac's program is about 8 weeks. I believe it's about $100/ day, so I hope to take advantage of their payment plan options.*

I think it would go a long way for you two (since you're the closest thing he has to parents/mentors, and because he respects and loves you immensely) to let him know that in order for him to return to work, he must complete this program. His life has been centered around justification and his disease has already forced him to call Argo several times to check up on things. His disease will use almost any excuse to not focus on his recovery and focus on trying to get him back to Argo (which gives him much easier access to drugs and alcohol).

Thankfully(?), he chose a dealer/drug that was free to him, otherwise, I'm sure we'd be in financial ruins. I only mention this because he is supposed to be taking medications that block the response and craving for certain opioids. But if he's not fully in recovery, his disease will force him to switch drugs.

Thanks for your help with this.

ps - I've also found Al-Anon to be very helpful in dealing with the stress involved in living with an addict. If you'd like any information, let me know.

* * * *

Scott flew back to D.C. on August 1, 2011.

One of the best decisions I ever made was to tell him that he couldn't live at home when he returned. He was angry about that, but he found a room to rent near Lincoln Park. I wish I could say my decision was completely altruistic and that I made it because I knew we both needed space to work on our own programs. That part was true, of course, and I believed it whole-heartedly. But part of me was just pissed. I don't think I was trying to get back at him. I think I was just trying to get back some of the power over me that I had ceded to him.

Even though it was hard to continue taking care of everything on my own, I really needed our home to remain a calm and safe space for Ara and me. And Scott was anything but calm when he returned from Florida. It's often said that a person becomes emotionally stunted at the age they became an addict. That's why there are so many newly sober "teenage" adults running around! Scott was all that and then some. At the age of thirty-three, he was behaving like a fourteen-year-old "dry drunk." [program speak for somebody who is sober—not drinking—but not in recovery]

I can't imagine what being sober must have been like for him. For the first time since he was a teenager, he was experiencing life with no buffer. He was also going through back-to-back withdrawal episodes known as PAWS (Post-Acute Withdrawal Syndrome) for the first several months he was home.

But, even knowing how much Scott was suffering didn't make being around him any easier. I had prayed for him to get sober for so long and with every ounce of my being. It never occurred to me that things would actually be *worse* than they were before.

He looked different, too. During inpatient treatment, he had gained weight and started smoking again. He had also found a new deodorant or cologne, so he smelled really different, too. And he had shaved his beard. None of this was a big deal, but it did create a big disconnect for me. Scott looked like a different person, and clearly he had been changed in treatment. And yet, here he was, still so angry, still acting as if *I* had done something to *him*!

If I had been stronger or more detached, perhaps I could have seen how terrified he was underneath all the changes. But I couldn't. Everything was still so raw and scary for me, too.

After five turbulent days back in D.C.—we could barely be in the same room together without getting into a screaming match—Scott agreed that going to an outpatient treatment center was a good idea. Thank God.

* * * *

August 5, 2011
Dear Shaaren,
> *I never meant to hurt you and am so sorry that I did. I have placed calls to both Kolmac and Washington Hospital Center to continue my treatment. I could not decide which thing to give you now and which thing to wait and give you on your birthday, so I decided to give them both to you now.*
> *Happy Birthday!*
> *I love you so much and I am so sorry!*

* * * *

Inpatient treatment in Florida had done what it was supposed to. It had broken him down. But because of the limits on our health insurance coverage, it didn't have time to finish the project. Kolmac, we hoped, would build him back up.

I learned about the Kolmac Clinic from several people including Scott's therapist and our friends, Mari and Brian. Kolmac had been around for over thirty years treating alcohol and drug addiction on an outpatient basis. It had a number of locations in the nearby Maryland suburbs as well as one in D.C. Its treatment program had three phases: detoxification, intense outpatient, and continuing care. Since Scott had already gone through detox down in Florida, he could start in the outpatient phase. Outpatients went to Kolmac, Monday through Friday, for three hours of group therapy and education. The number of sessions per week was gradually reduced every week. After eight weeks (totaling about twenty or thirty sessions) patients would transition into the continuing care phase where they would attend once-a-week group therapy sessions.

And I was continuing to work my own program.

On top of Al-anon, *I* continued to rely on my Twitter #xa recovery community to help me—"a meeting in my pocket" for whenever I needed it.

I was also continuing my own therapy through all these changes, and that was essential. I loved Al-Anon, but sometimes I just needed to tell my story without worrying about my detachment. To be heard and understood without having my story rewritten or dismissed. And, having *somebody else* acknowledge the crap factor of being married to a man who was a complete asshole a lot of the time, was extremely healing.

CHAPTER 32

Scott

My return to D.C. was not what I thought it would be. When I got off the plane at BWI, there were no "Welcome Home!" or "We Missed You!" signs. In fact, no one even came to the airport to meet me. I had to take the train from BWI to Union Station. And then I had to face head on the destruction I had caused. My wife had found out all my dirty secrets, and boy did she hate me! Here I was thinking all would be forgiven and forgotten. After all, I did the right thing. I got help. But before I even left Florida to come home, Shaaren made it clear that I had to find somewhere else to live—at least for a while. It was non-negotiable.

I was lucky enough to touch base with Tom at a meeting, who lived on the Hill and was going through his own recovery. He generously opened up his home to me for the first couple of weeks. After that I found a room to rent on a month-to-month basis also on Capitol Hill. So here I was, back home but homeless (more or less), with a wife who hated me, and I still didn't understand why.

The greatest insult was that Shaaren forbade me from going to my own bar! Who the fuck did she think she was telling me I couldn't even return to work in my own bar? I didn't understand that it wasn't mainly about being around the alcohol. Rather, it was the stress of work that my counselors and Shaaren wanted me to ease back into.

Looking back, I don't know why these conditions came as such a surprise to me. I had been told when I was in treatment that I'd have to find another kind of job and that I couldn't continue to work around alcohol. They told me that everything I had been used to in my life would have to change. I was supposed to continue working on myself, not working at a bar. But I found it easy to forget what I didn't want to hear. And besides, I had just gotten out of treatment! I was sober! I was fixed!

In fact, I was still a complete mess. A dry drunk and still an asshole. I had built up huge resentments and had no tools to deal with them. Sure, I had learned a little during my inpatient treatment. But were twenty days of treatment really supposed to cure twenty years of addiction? *I* sure thought so.

I was excellent at manipulating program speak to meet my own needs "I'm SUPPOSED to be working on myself" in order to substitute being selfish in my choices for actually working on myself. "I can only control myself" I would yell at Shaaren to assert my control in situations where my ideas weren't going over very well.

I was a time bomb those first five days back in D.C. I had built up so much resentment and hate. I couldn't understand why Shaaren wasn't happy to see me, why she was pressuring me so hard to continue my treatment. I was confused and alone and I just wanted to get my old life back.

In fact, I was pretty much the same as I was before I left: confrontational, argumentative, controlling, and filled with anger. Except this time I had no crutch to fall back on. Nothing to numb me. Plus, I was constantly getting my arm twisted by my wife (whom I was determined not to listen to) and a number of other people to continue treatment as an outpatient. Finally, I took the advice of Tom and some people in my AA group and decided I would go to outpatient treatment at the D.C. branch of the Kolmac Clinic.

About a week after getting back from Florida, I started going to Kolmac's night program. The clinic was located on the sixth floor of an office building on K Street, N.W., in downtown D.C. The program was three hours a night, five nights a week. On any particular night, anywhere from twelve to twenty people would show up. The first hour was check in with our two counselors. We'd sit in a circle and they'd go around the room asking us how we were doing. They wanted to know if we had any triggers, that is, something that made you think about drinking or using. During check in, we could talk to the counselor about relapses or anything else we were having problems with. And we were asked to suggest a topic for the next part of the meeting.

The second hour was a group discussion. We talked about issues people had brought up in the first hour, or anything else that was on our minds. There were only a couple of rules: no cross talk and you could only talk about your own experience, not give other people advice.

During the third hour there was a speaker—a different one each night. One topic might be chemical dependency and how it changes your brain. We also had speakers who talked about feelings and learning to recognize the signs your body gives that could help you avoid stressful situations that could lead to a relapse. On another night we might have an AA meeting and people came in to tell their stories. Most people in the group liked these discussions.

The people at Kolmac were very different than the people at BHOPB in Florida. No one seemed as desperate as those I had been with in inpatient treatment. That was probably because any extreme cases like me had already gone through inpatient treatment and were now continuing as outpatients. It didn't take me long to figure out that some of the people in the group were not serious about staying clean. Perhaps like me in my twenties, they were there because a court required it, or because they were trying to make a good impression with the courts. The others were older professionals, mostly attorneys, and most of them had alcohol problems. And there were no other restaurant workers.

This life was so new to me. At first, I didn't know what to do with my time when I wasn't at Kolmac. It was extremely difficult to stay sober. My inclination was simply to pick up where I had left off when I went to Florida. I was fortunate that Kolmac did random testing for drugs. They also put everyone on Antabuse, a drug that makes you extremely sick if you drink while you're taking it. This is true even for food that has alcohol in it. Boy, did I light up like a lobster one night when I ordered the crab soup at Argo. I knew it had sherry in it, but I figured it would have cooked off. My face flushed, I was burning up and sweating like hell. I can only imagine what would have happened if I had tried to drink while on Antabuse.

CHAPTER 33

Shaaren

Addiction is unpredictable. It affects each person quite differently. Scott became a monster, but he didn't *look* really sick until the very end, at least to me, anyway. Some addicts have a much more physical reaction, wasting away or gaining weight, losing teeth or hair. So it's not surprising that each addict's recovery process would be different too.

I'm sure this is accurate for many addicts, but Scott had two major types of withdrawal. The first or acute stage of withdrawal—when the addict has just stopped using—generally lasts only a few days or weeks. It is mostly physical. The second stage of withdrawal—known as Post-Acute Withdrawal Syndrome or PAWS—can also be quite different depending on, for example, the drug abused, the age of the addict when he started or stopped using, and how long he used the drug. There are still some physical symptoms such as headaches, and feeling and looking sick. But there are a lot more emotional and psychological symptoms. Scott's PAWS was really bad. I wonder if the *severity* of PAWS symptoms depends on how long and what substances a person was using. I haven't found a lot of research on it. (We codependents love to do research! It makes us feel like we're somehow in control.)

Unfortunately, all my research didn't stop Scott's PAWS from being awful. I would describe it as a kind of chemical recalibration of his brain, which was trying gradually to start returning to normal. Scott had absolutely no control over when a PAWS episode would begin. He'd be fine one day and the next day he'd wake up feeling tired, irritable, moody, and suffering from headaches. He actually looked physically ill as well, with dark circles under his eyes. In fact, he looked kind of like he did when he was using. And, typical Scott, he'd forget that just because he was in a bad mood didn't mean he always had to act like it. His PAWS was cyclical and each episode would last about four days.

I'm guessing that during inpatient treatment in Florida and for the first month afterwards, Scott was probably going through almost continuous PAWS cycles. By the fall, however, the amount of time between the cycles began to lengthen—first by a week, then two weeks, then four weeks, then a month and a half, then two months. The time between each episode was not quite doubling, but it was definitely increasing—a good sign.

During each PAWS cycle, it felt like the old Scott was back. The one who was horrible to be around. The one who was sure the world was out to get him. The one who felt that any question or suggestion was an unreasonable demand. He would constantly reprise his role as an asshole. During one PAWS episode, he actually honked at the officer in the police car in front of us who didn't respond as quickly as Scott thought he should have when the traffic light changed to green!

At first, neither one of us would realize that another round of PAWS was starting. Scott would be fine one day and just a hot mess the next. By the third day of an episode, I would figure out what was happening, but it didn't stop me from fighting back. Now that there were some moments of calmness, the hell of PAWS seemed even worse! I'd allow myself to get into stupid arguments with him instead of following the rules: The addict is like a goldfish. Would you argue with a goldfish? If somebody is watching, who looks stupid? The goldfish? Or you? And, that when he was ranting, I was supposed to imagine him in a straightjacket. Or that I should picture him with the word "sick" written on his forehead. It would help me not engage.

I finally started tracking the episodes on a calendar and I'd add a note to myself: Look for next PAWS around "x" date. I couldn't do anything to stop it, but at least I could prepare myself for it. That helped immensely.

I should clarify that the tracking helped *me* a lot. Scott had always believed that his anger was justified, that his feelings were facts, and that when he was in a bad mood it was because "we had done things to him." I've come to understand that addicts are often the biggest codependents.

Like many addicts, Scott rarely wanted to acknowledge that something he was going through was actually quite common. He preferred to believe that nobody had suffered as much as he had!

I, on the other hand, found great comfort in knowing that the changes I was experiencing in myself, living with an addict, were normal and that most other people faced with the same situation did the exact same things.

It took a full six months for Scott to begin to calm down a little bit. And it was probably a full year before he began to resemble a "normal" adult. Then, even with his new skills, a PAWS episode would come along and knock us both on our butts. Although I had probably read it somewhere, I'm not sure I fully absorbed the fact that even though individual episodes of PAWS occur less and less frequently as the addict's brain recovers, they can continue for ten or more years.

Fortunately, there were positive developments as well. Around the six- or eight- month mark of Scott's sobriety, I started to see that even though each PAWS episode was still awful, Scott would have a kind of cognitive leap afterwards. I could almost see his brain healing, literally growing new connections. He was able to verbalize new concepts—especially in the empathy department—more than he ever had before.

I don't mean to make Scott sound like a toddler during this process, but in a way he was. He certainly acted like a stubborn, tantrum-throwing two year old a lot! As annoying and horrible as it was, this made sense to me. He had started using alcohol and drugs when he was very young and his brain wasn't fully developed. And then he continued to alter his brain chemistry in a negative way for twenty years.

His brain wasn't the only brain that surprised me. I was floored by my own feelings after Scott's return. My long-running resentments started to creep back in when he came home. I mean, he had just had an entire twenty-one days to work on himself. Near the beach in Florida, no less. Sure, I knew treatment wasn't all sitting around eating peeled grapes. But between taking care of Ara and the house and Argo and everything else that came up while he was away, I was exhausted. And it didn't get any better when he returned. Of course, I realized I was the one who had told him when he got back to stay away from work and continue to focus on himself. But it was still hard for me. It seemed like such a luxury to be able to take weeks off at a time. I couldn't even remember a life like that.

He got to go to therapy, the chiropractor, the gym, rehab and AA meetings. I was green with envy and quite lacking in compassion. But *of course* he "got" to go to these things. He was horribly deficient as a human being and needed them so he could begin to function on the most basic level. And *of course* I understood all this—intellectually. But I still longed for some time to care for myself.

* * * *

    August 25, 2011—We're all getting sick and yet it's harder for him. We're all busy and yet he complains the loudest. He has an entire TEAM looking out for him and still gets to go to the gym and go tanning. TANNING?! I want somebody to take care of ME! I want Scott to say, "Wow. You're doing a great job, Shaaren. I'm really proud of and impressed by you."

* * * *

I assume my reaction is pretty common. Unlike some families, we weren't spending an exorbitant amount of money on treatment because we had good health insurance. But even when there isn't a great drain on personal finances, somebody is always left behind to continue picking up the slack and trying to hold their lives together. In our case, that was me.

Another thing I didn't expect to feel was annoyance. The more Scott changed for the better and became the man I was always encouraging him to be—somebody who exercised, meditated, didn't do drugs—the more annoyed I got. Of course, I was thrilled with the changes. But it took some adjustment. I would hear Scott praising the benefits of exercise to non-exercisers as if he personally had just discovered a new planet. I'd be all, "Um, hai hello? Haven't I been espousing the virtues of exercise to you for *years*?!"

Even at the time, I knew my response was petty. Yet there it was. I guess the real issue was that despite our obvious partnership on many levels—our marriage, the amazing kid we shared, our hard work and commitment to the Argonaut—by the time Scott left for treatment in Florida, our relationship had become incredibly adversarial and contentious. So now it seemed strange for him to be agreeing with me. He had been progressively isolating and blaming me for everything that went wrong for so long that this sudden switch to acknowledging the benefits of "my" way was quite a change.

And trust. I still didn't trust him. But not just in the ways one might think. Of course, I would still get suspicious and worried that I was being lied to. But it was more than that. In the past, Scott only agreed with me, or was nice around me, or would do something nice for me because he had gotten himself "in trouble." Then he would over-compensate to try and get himself "out of trouble." After he got back from Florida, try as I might to stop myself, my first reaction to him doing something nice was still my old response: "What. Did. You. Do." More of a statement than a question. It was a real struggle to accept him at his word.

I also wasn't prepared for having such a visceral reactions to some pretty benign stuff Scott would do when he first got back. Like using mouthwash with alcohol in it! Just the smell of alcohol on Scott's breath made me nauseous. It took a lot of willpower for me not to yell, "You asshole, what are you thinking?" But my body wasn't as cooperative. My pulse would race, dread would fill the pit of my stomach, and I felt like I was about to throw up. I'm not sure this kind of gut response will ever completely disappear. But at least we could solve this particular problem by not buying mouthwash that contained alcohol. If only everything were that simple.

Memories of Scott's old behaviors kept coming back to me. When he was using, Scott used to yell "I just need to clear my head!" all the time. Even though he never said it anymore, just thinking about it made me feel ill. I suppose the thought itself was a trigger that took me back to the past. It reminded me that he never actually wanted to "clear" his head. What he really wanted was to get fucked up. Or get more fucked up than he already was. I'm not sure he consciously thought of it that way, but because he had no coping skills, anything that was stressful (real, imagined, or created by him to "cause" stress) was a great excuse to use alcohol or drugs. He used those words to push me and Ara away and continue to isolate himself. He was telling us that we were too much of a burden and that he couldn't be around us. Not the stuff of fairy tales.

Since I had spent a lot of the time that *I* was really ill, snooping and searching for drugs, just opening the middle console in the car, or doing laundry sometimes caused me incredible anxiety. Even though I knew he was clean, just the thought of finding something was enough to cause me panic.

One thing that took me aback as Scott continued to recover was truly out of his control. Sometimes, after working out or meditating, he would look like he was high. His pupils were dilated and he seemed like he was kind of out of his body. Of course, as a runner, I knew that was a perfectly normal state that can happen to anyone. But when I saw Scott like that, I had to consciously remind myself that he was not using again.

Slowly, day by day, he started to get better. And day by day I did, too.

Scott moved back in with Ara and me on November 1, 2011. He'd been on the couch since the beginning of the year, then treatment, then his own apartment, so this was a pretty big deal. Far from perfect, but a pretty big deal.

CHAPTER 34

Shaaren

I really struggled with staying in the present moment. Not ruining every day worrying about what *could* or *might* happen. I didn't do my worrying in the "normal" way, though. I often didn't want good things happening because I was terrified that something bad would then happen to "take it all away." To somehow "balance the scales."

With the help of therapy I was getting much better at recognizing my tendency to obsess over every little thing—and then talking myself out of it. But I still had a long way to go. My therapist explained that this hyper-vigilance was a normal reaction, a form of PTSD (Post-Traumatic Stress Disorder) or anxiety disorder after all the traumas of the last few years.

On top of Scott's irrational and unpredictable addict behavior, there had been the ordeal of the Argonaut's terrible June 2010 fire and its aftermath.

Plus, our attorney had always told us, "If you have employees, you will have employee problems." He knew what he was talking about. We endured three separate and particularly vengeful attacks from former employees—two fraudulent lawsuits and one fraudulent attempt to have Ara taken from us. All three attacks ultimately failed, but the experiences were traumatic to say the least. All this just meant that I had a lot more recovering to do.

Scott didn't suffer from the same kind of reaction to our circumstances as I did and couldn't really relate. But eventually, he could at least acknowledge—if not understand—what I was going through. It was a great comfort when he said, "I need to remember that you process things differently than I do. You feel *everything*."

After Scott's return, we both worked really hard to be as honest as we could with Ara about her Daddy's illness. Both of us truly believe that we are only as sick as our secrets. I didn't want our daughter to internalize anything about Scott's addiction, knowing that, like me, she feels everything intensely. I wanted her to focus on empathy and compassion, not codependence. And use her powers for good.

With some distance, I could even joke a little about my (and my daughter's) intense experiencing. When Ara would get upset about something that wasn't really a problem, I could say, "Meh. *This* is not a crisis. Have you learned *nothing* from our lives? *Haven't you been paying attention?* It can get *So Much Worse!*"

There is nothing quite like enduring a crisis—or going through recovery—to put things into perspective. I remembered how Scott and I had longed for 2010 to begin because it "couldn't possibly be worse than 2009." In hindsight, I'm not sure what was so bad about 2009. As I recall, our car was broken into several times, maybe even stolen. And our attempt to refinance our house was rejected. But certainly nothing happened that would qualify as a crisis *now*.

Mostly, in the days and months after Scott returned from inpatient treatment, he and I were just trying to work on ourselves. To keep our sides of the street clean. I had always exercised (sometimes to an unhealthy degree), but now I did it to keep myself sane. It was the biggest part of my self-care plan and I worked out at least five days a week. I'm sure I could have functioned without it, but I was definitely a better person, mom, wife, boss, and everything else after a good jog and some weights.

Scott was going to Kolmac regularly—initially five days each week, then a continuing care schedule of once a week. He was also working out and meditating. He could get away with skipping exercise or even not going to AA meetings for a couple of days. But if he skipped meditating, all bets were off. Mostly, it was just important for him to keep a routine.

They say addicts relapse when something goes into their mouths and Al-Anons relapse when something comes out.

In the community, there is some division about what constitutes a relapse. Some people think a solitary incident is only a lapse, and a longer one would be a relapse. I tend to think they're both relapses, but I'm not sure it matters.

Scott had two types of relapse. The first occurred when he didn't attend to his recovery (Kolmac, exercise, and meditation). He would start to get that "thinking problem" (the first part of relapse) and become weighed down by resentments and stress. If he didn't immediately refocus on his recovery, the "drinking problem" (the second part of relapse) was a very short jump from there.

Scott had two drinking relapses during the December after he returned from treatment. At some point, he had decided to quit smoking again and wanted to see if hypnosis would help. During the introductory session, the hypnotist claimed that he could make a suggestion under hypnosis so that Scott could have a glass of wine without any problems. When Scott told me this, I couldn't believe it. What irresponsibility on the part of the hypnotist! Of course, Scott latched onto the idea like grim death and convinced himself that it was possible. "My problem was really pills," he'd say. Sure enough, after only a few weeks with this "thinking problem," he took a drink.

But relapse is often a part of recovery. In fact, it can teach the addict more about his disease than the first months of sobriety do. Although it may sound counterintuitive at first, the good part about relapse is that the addict usually picks up with his drug of choice right where he left off. This was certainly true for Scott, who fell right on his ass. Hopefully, in the future, he would remember that he didn't want to go out there again. The scary part about relapse is that although every addict has another drunk inside himself, he might not have another recovery.

I, of course, had my own kind of relapse. It was when I once again started telling Scott how to live his life. Asking myself two sets of questions sometimes helped me avoid relapsing into my old behaviors:

— Does it need to be said? Does it need to be said now? Does it need to be said by me?
— Is there a problem? Whose problem is it? Can I fix it? Who asked me to?

Sometimes, that wasn't enough and I quite literally had to clamp my hands over my mouth to keep my unsolicited opinions from coming out.

About a year after Scott got sober, we were having dinner with friends and looking at some photos of Scott shortly before he went into treatment. In one especially, he looks just awful. Tired, hollow, unhealthy.

Like a junkie.

I turned to Scott and said, "I just can't believe I couldn't see how sick you were."

He looked at me and said, "Well, you were sick too."

How true.

I try not to worry too much about Scott relapsing—for a couple of reasons. First, there is nothing I can do about it. But also, the thought of him ending up back where he had been is just too devastating. Plus, relapse is scary. Often, people overdose because they jump right back in to where they left off, but their bodies no longer have the same tolerance. It always lands me in a very unhealthy place if I obsess over it. But I did (and do) think about it enough to know that we will *never* really be out of the woods.

In some ways, being associated with the restaurant world is a great reminder for Scott of where he doesn't want to be. Sometimes, we both see people at their absolute worst. Drunk, belligerent, mean. Or, we see people who remind him who he doesn't want to be anymore. People whom we always thought were single because they're always at Argo - and later find out they're married? Or have kids at home? I think that helps Scott stay sober. And the dying. Even on our little strip of H Street, with only a handful of restaurants and watering holes, we've had four drug- or alcohol-related deaths in just seven years. Those numbers keep him sober, too.

We both know that addiction would mean a lifetime of vigilance for Scott. And not just in the most obvious ways like attending to basics—not letting himself get too hungry, angry, lonely or tired; going to his continuing care meetings at the Kolmac Clinic; and exercising and meditating. It meant watching out for stuff most of us don't even have to think about. Like telling every oral hygienist, dentist, doctor, and ER nurse that he's an addict and can't have a non-local painkiller. Like worrying about meals or recipes that call for alcohol and avoiding many over-the-counter medications.

But we both believe he could do this. One day at a time.

CHAPTER 35

Scott

I wish I could say that inpatient treatment at The Cottages and outpatient treatment at the Kolmac Clinic solved all my problems, but they didn't. What these treatment centers did do was give me some tools to at least *start facing* my problems. In the past, I was in complete denial about the pain I had caused. Besides enforcing almost a month of total sobriety, the inpatient program in Florida introduced me to meditation and mindfulness practices and got me thinking about caring for my body as well as my brain. Back in D.C. at the Kolmac Clinic, I was given a chance to learn skills I would need to be productive for the rest of my (sober) life.

Although Shaaren had banned me from going to Argo when I first got back from Florida, I had every intention of returning to my restaurant as soon as possible. In those first few early days, before I started going to Kolmac's outpatient program at night, evenings and other downtimes were especially hard. I remember stopping by Argo a few times and visiting with Shaaren and Ara while they were having their nightly dinner there.

The evenings were easier once I started going to Kolmac. I learned about the relapse cycle and how to determine what my triggers were. Kolmac also taught me how to recognize my body's signals before they became an issue. And how to deal with stressors (people, places, things). Basically, Kolmac was offering outpatient addicts like me a crash course in life.

I discovered I could actually string together some good days. I was finally learning about feelings. But I was still an asshole a lot of the time.

I still held onto many of my old resentments and much of the time I still believed I was the victim. In my personal life, progress repairing the damage I had done was slow. I knew Shaaren really hated me. But I couldn't grasp *why* she hated me so much. I had built up so much resentment toward her. Learning to process information that could help me understand how someone else might feel was quite new to me. I had always lied about everything. In fact, I would tell a lie without even thinking about it. There were just so many things I was scared or ashamed to tell the truth about. So I never told the truth—to myself or anyone else. I think that, at some point, all the lies I told became the truth as I saw it. It is hard to recover from such a life of lies. And it is hard to build trust again with someone you have lied to for so long. To make matters worse, I still couldn't stop myself from getting mad at Shaaren for everything. I'd get mad that she was mad. And I'd get mad that she didn't trust me. This lack of trust was almost the last nail in the coffin when it came to saving our relationship.

How little Shaaren trusted me really sunk in when I came back from Florida. I knew that she wasn't going to let me live in my own house or go back to work at Argo right away. But she was also setting the schedule for when I could spend time with my own daughter. I was furious at the time, but now I know that she was being smart. I needed to earn back the trust. I am grateful that my daughter was too young to understand much of what was going on during this whole period. While I was using, I had always tried to over-compensate with Ara and be super-nice to her. I think I did this to deflect any blame from myself and make it seem like Shaaren was always the one at fault. I had to feel my way to a whole new relationship with both my wife and my daughter.

Although my drug use in high school had quickly put an end to the constant talking that earned me the nickname "Motor Mouth" as a kid, it probably increased my need to be always on the move. I could barely stay still for a few minutes, much less sit with myself. Even with some basic meditation and mindfulness skills I had learned during inpatient treatment at The Cottages, I found I was still having problems just sitting with myself. And why not? If I hated myself when I was abusing drugs and alcohol, I sure as hell hated myself even more now that I was sober.

Being sober for the first time, I finally began to see the destruction I had caused throughout my life. The fact that I could have saved my own mother's life hurt the most. I thought about what her life could have been if I had given her a kidney. I thought about all the things she could have done. About all her talents that were never realized. I could not block out all the "what ifs" and "if onlys." Sobriety was forcing me to start feeling things and seeing things. One of the things I could now see was how selfish and self-absorbed I had been. But I had no idea about, or experience with, how to deal with any sort of emotion, good or bad.

When I first returned to DC, I had tried to continue meditating. I found that doing it on my own was a very slow and uncertain process. Guided meditation had worked for me in Florida because it gave me the sense that I was doing it right. Fortunately, back in D.C. I found a website (fragrantheart.com) that had a whole bunch of audio guided meditations. I started out with the very short ones and gradually moved on to longer ones. As I got more comfortable with meditation, I also found it easier to just be with myself. I would sit or lie down and listen to guided meditations, especially the ones on loving kindness—the practice of empathy.

Loving kindness meditation practice helped me start thinking about other people and myself in a positive, loving way. This was quite a discovery. Many people dealing with addiction—including me—have a problem with love. I think meditating on loving kindness helped me realize that you can't truly love anyone else if you don't love yourself. I realized how long I had hated myself. I always thought that changing my surroundings, changing my look, changing everything on the outside would make me happy. But you can never be happy if you hate yourself. Meditation provided a way to look within myself and begin to make changes. It opened up my life. It helped me change the way I thought and felt about myself. I even felt a little pride about the person I was becoming.

Meditating also helped me begin to process my past experiences. I realized that, although I couldn't change the past, I could learn from it. When I first got sober, I was unable to sit still. I didn't know how to turn my brain off. I was full of negative thoughts and insecurities. For so many years, alcohol had given me the confidence to talk to people and be comfortable in social settings. Now that I was sober, I had no clue how to talk with people. I was uncomfortable in just about every social interaction.

The irony wasn't lost on me. My whole previous adult life in the bar and restaurant world had revolved around being social. Meditation helped me gain confidence in my sober self so that I could have conversations with people again and confidence in my decision-making process. When I fell so low that treatment was the only option, I had to change every aspect of my life. Just like every other addict, I had to start over. It began with changing my thought processes and finding something new to believe in. Some people find God, some people find AA and NA programs. I found meditation and mindfulness.

While I was in therapy at Kolmac, Jen, the clinical director there, gave me a book called *Dharma Punx: A Memoir* by Noah Levine[iv]. At AA meetings I had gone to, people were always talking about having a "spiritual awakening." [program speak for a specific event that has enough power to allow the addict to break away from their addiction] I just didn't get it. But after reading Levine's book, I did.

I already knew about Noah Levine from the "Meditate and Destroy" documentary I had seen during treatment in Florida. Levine is the son of Buddhist teacher Stephen Levine. In *Dharma Punx,* he writes about his teenage years, which were filled with drugs, violence, and multiple suicide attempts. His substance abuse had started early—at age six he began smoking marijuana. He finally ended up in a padded detox cell in juvenile prison eleven years later. Facing the possibility at age seventeen of spending his life in prison, Levine says he thought, "Maybe I'll try dad's hippie meditation bullshit." Each person has "a different doorway to dharma or spiritual practice," Levine says. "Suffering is a doorway. [It] opened me to the possibility of trying meditation." While incarcerated, Levine saw for the first time how the practice his father had taught him gave him the tools to relieve the fear and uncertainty that ruled his life.

I could completely identify with Noah Levine and the winding path he had taken. His book got me reading more books about Buddhism, meditation, and mindfulness. One day, while I was sitting in an AA meeting meditating, I had a vision of the Buddha sitting under the Bodhi tree. At the time I thought, "This is kind of weird." But it also seemed like a powerful message. Later that day, I was reading a book on Buddhism that talked about people having this same vision. It blew my mind.

And that was *my* spiritual awakening.

Meditation and mindfulness became a huge part of my recovery. It occurred to me that these two practices should be taught to kids at an early age. What was the point of getting impatient and pissed off all the time? So many people were so self-absorbed and didn't appreciate the true beauty of their lives. Sometimes, during or right after meditating, I would feel like I was seeing the world in HD. And I knew I had only begun to scratch the surface of Buddhism and mindfulness practice. Of course, I still got impatient and pissed off sometimes. I had (and have) good days and bad days, just like everyone else. Especially when I was hungry or tired, my default mode was always: I'm the wronged party. That was something I had to work on—mainly by being more aware and taking better care of myself so I didn't reach that hungry or tired state so often. But the big difference—the bottom line—was that I was no longer pissed off *all* the time.

Another important difference in my life was that now I went to the gym every day. When I was drinking and using drugs, there was no way in hell you would ever catch me in a gym. Fuck that! But now I *had* to go there. It was (and is) a huge stress reliever for me. But it wasn't only about relieving stress and improving my mood. I was surprised—but not disappointed—to find that working out gave me some of the rush that my body used to get from drugs. It was a win-win. I was sober and in the best shape I had ever been in my life with a healthier body, mind and spirit.

As my intense outpatient treatment at Kolmac was tapering off to fewer meetings each week, I gradually started adding hours to my work week at Argo. Eventually, under Kolmac's continuing care plan, I was only going to one meeting each week. Shaaren and I tried to make sure I wouldn't take on too much, too fast at Argo and get myself in a situation that would trigger a relapse.

I was still angry a lot. But slowly, my thought process was changing. I started treating the Argonaut more as a job and less as a social party. But I won't deny that those first six months of recovery were hard. Major resentments welled up as I watched everyone else drink and have a good time. Why could they drink and I couldn't? I felt very awkward in social situations now. After all, my social life had always involved drugs and alcohol. For eighteen years—more than half my life—and for all of my adult life, I had always been high or drinking whenever I was in a social setting. Shaaren asked me a few times if she should quit drinking around me. But how was that fair? I just pretended it didn't bother me. But some days it seemed like the only thing I was doing was fighting the constant urge to use, especially alcohol. I still blamed my addiction mainly on the painkillers I had been taking for years. That meant I didn't have to face the fact that alcohol was also part of my addiction. Can you imagine? Given all the stories I've just told and I could still convince myself I didn't have a problem!

With this kind of fuzzy and self-serving thinking, it's not surprising that I relapsed. Twice. Both times with alcohol. My first relapse was during a holiday party that our local firehouse—the one that had fought our fire—had at Argo. I was managing the event and used it as an excuse to throw back a couple. I hated the holidays. I had always used them as an excuse to get wasted. To forget. This was my first holiday season sober. The first time I had to relive the pain of my mother's death sober. Only a couple of weeks later I relapsed again during Argo's big, combination birthday, holiday, and staff party. Thankfully, both times that I relapsed, I didn't have just one or two beers. Typical me, I went all out—beer, shots, and quite a hangover.

Despite the relapses, I still consider my sobriety date to be July 12, 2011. Maybe if I had stayed out there [program speak for relapsing] longer, I would have started the clock over, but these two relapses have been such an important part of maintaining sobriety. I know that if I had been able to control my drinking during those two relapses, I would have set my recovery back. I would have continued to drink under the illusion that I had some control. And even scarier, who knows if I ever would have found my way back to recovery.

Through meditation, I learned a form of self-hypnosis that has really helped me stay sober. I taught myself how to have a counter-thought that would serve as a new trigger. Every time I thought about drinking, I would have an automatic thought that asked one simple question: "What's the point?" This question created a kind of red flag in my head. It made me stop and think about what I was doing. So many people relapse by second nature. They don't even stop for a minute to think.

Gradually, I stopped thinking about drinking as much. I made sure I meditated every day for fifteen or twenty minutes at a time. I made plans to attend an Insight Meditation group meeting sometime soon. I worked out. I was taking care of myself.

CHAPTER 36

Shaaren

I think the biggest issue I was still facing was trust. How could I trust Scott after all the lies?

The answer was...slowly.

Once he started to calm down, I would let him care for Ara by himself again. Or I'd let him take her somewhere—just the two of them. Part of my problem before was that I always believed what he said but I didn't look at his actions. Now, I watched what he did. Was it what he said he was going to do? Could I count on him?

As more and more days of reliability and responsibility replaced the old memories, trust got easier. But I still struggled with it. I figured it would take a while to get it back. Or maybe it would never be the same as before.

I did start to believe I could count on Scott to be the same person nearly every day—to be present, to be rational, and to be able to deal with my emotions. In short, to be a partner. Even though we had been together since 2005, it was like we were starting a brand new relationship. But this time it was for *real*. And this time was scarier because there was so much more to lose.

What helped me heal me the most, though, was when Scott began to acknowledge the truth of the past. As an adoptee, I was already sensitive to the rewriting of my story and the denial of my experience. Most adoptees have had our origins and first families redacted or deleted, changed or falsified on whatever documents we may be in possession of – erasing our pasts. And many adoptees have complicated feelings about our adoptions, but we are unable to voice them, because most people identify with adoptive parents and agencies. When Scott would minimize, dismiss or distort what was happening, it was particularly hard for me. He would never admit or concede participation, let alone guilt. Even after he became sober, he wasn't yet strong enough to face the pain he had caused others. As more time has passed, however, he was able to accept responsibility for the devastation he had wreaked on our family. That validation—acknowledging the truth of the past—was so healing for me.

Ara, who was now five, had begun to forget the specifics of what her Daddy used to be like – yelling or throwing things, or being absent. Of course, there were little things she still did and said that were reminders of that earlier time. She still called our bedroom "Momma's room" because, for almost a year, it really was mine alone. And she still called Scott's recovery professionals "special, special doctors." Sometimes, when we were talking to someone, we'd refer to Kolmac as Scott's "class." Every time that happened, Ara would always call us out in that loud and honest and hilarious way that only young children can do. "Daddy's not going to *class*," she'd announce. "He's going to *REHAB!*"

And, as two people who have lost mothers, we know that trauma lives in our cells and our memories, even if we can't actually recall the memories. One of the ways we have failed her is sometimes forgetting that lack of language or specific memory negates traumatic experience. There are things that trigger in Ara a visceral, emotional, and heartfelt reaction because of her loss, trauma, and grief that ever so occasionally will rise to the surface. They always catch us by surprise, and yet, of anyone, we should know better. In her little life, our losses are hers (she, too, has lost an entire Indian family, whom she misses terribly despite none of us ever having met, and a paternal grandmother), plus, the fire, the pain and uncertainty and chaos of living with an addict, and her father leaving her to go to treatment.

Thankfully, when these episodes occur, we talk her through it, we acknowledge and validate all of her feelings, and we just sit with her, letting the feelings of sadness wash over her without attempting to silence her narrative—even if it makes us uncomfortable, even if we want her to stop hurting, and even if we feel guilty about how we've come to be in this place.

This process helps her heal. And helping her heal, helps us heal.

As time went on and trust returned, the biggest and best thing we did to heal as a family was to have fun together. When Scott was sick he didn't ever want to be with us. In recovery, he actually started to enjoy being with us. He had more patience and was able to laugh with us. And, perhaps more importantly, we were able to laugh with him.

In illness we could never vacation together or, if we did, it went poorly. I'd find drugs, he'd sneak off and I couldn't find him, he'd be euphoric one day and a monster the next. In recovery, we went on family vacations!

On vacation in Aruba, July 19, 2013

In illness, he was so unfocused that work took forever. In recovery, he was much better at time management and would leave Argo much earlier to come home and be with us.

Even before knowing about Scott's drug abuse, I had hated prescription drugs. I slowed down my own recovery from the C-section when Ara was born because I was so reluctant to take my medication. Add Scott's drug abuse on top of that and my fears about pills became overwhelming.

I had to learn that there *is* a place for medication. Scott still needs a veritable pharmacy to function like a "normal" human being and I now realized that was okay. It was so much better than the self-prescribed and often illegal pharmacy he was using before.

The wonderful thing about reputable treatment centers like Kolmac and BHOPB is that they know their shit. They kept Scott on Lexapro (an anti-depressant), but changed everything else. Instead of Adderall, they gave him the non-stimulant Stratera for his ADHD. Instead of Klonopin, they gave him mood-stabilizing Gabapentin. Instead of leaving him to his own devices when it came to falling asleep, they gave him Remron.

There was a chance that, as Scott's brain healed, he would need fewer meds, smaller doses or different medications. But it was also possible that he would always need the same amount. Our daughter has asthma and, so far, she has needed both a long-term preventive medication, a rescue inhaler, and occasionally a nebulizer and steroids. Would we for a minute consider not treating her? Of course not. And it is no different when it comes to treating the chemical imbalances in Scott's brain.

Another thing I had to adjust was my view of how recovery should look. Because I had embraced Al-Anon so deeply in the beginning, I thought that AA was the only way for Scott to truly recover. I couldn't wrap my head around a recovery that didn't involve AA and I was highly skeptical of the ways Scott was keeping his sobriety.

Part of that was probably justified, given Scott's past, but a lot of it just required me to catch up. Just like there wasn't one right thing in Al-Anon, there wasn't going to be one right thing for all addicts. Working in a restaurant made AA meetings a nearly impossible model for Scott to embrace because many members do their best to avoid bars, liquor stores, etc. And yet, since I had never been to an AA meeting, I didn't understand that. Now, I realize that 1) I'm not in charge of his recovery and 2) whatever keeps him sober and in recovery is the best model for him. It's not for me to decide which path is the right one. (EVEN THOUGH I MIGHT WANT TO.)

I should also add that even though I know AA wasn't the solution for Scott, I am eternally grateful to them. And for that reason, I will not stick up my nose at what has worked so well for so many, what has been the only hope for millions of families for decades, and what has previously been the only cure for this disease with no cure. And which did so at a time when there were no anti-craving medications, no dual-diagnosis and alternate treatments, no therapies, no harm reduction and no end in sight except institutionalization, prison, or death.

And forgiveness. How does forgiveness work for families living with an addict? I know that we are supposed to forgive for ourselves. That holding onto rage and resentments is like taking poison and expecting the other person to get sick, but…I'm not good at it. It's hard for me to forget and it's hard for me to let go. It has taken time (SERIOUS, SERIOUS TIME) for me to start moving past everything that has happened to us.

Writing this book has been extremely therapeutic. There are things that Scott hasn't been able to say to me face to face (about the past, about his regrets, about his apologies) that he can communicate to me only through writing. In the beginning of Scott's recovery, all I wanted, in desperation, was an "I'm sorry" over and over and over again. But, I've since realized that living amends is much stronger than an "I'm sorry" and quickly moving on. Living amends is behavior change.

But, despite its therapeutic nature, it's difficult to write my truth, and think about my own guilt and embarrassment. It's really scary knowing others will read it. And, it's hard to look back on those times.

I'm so glad that we've been writing this down, though, working through things, and elongating the process, because I'm starting to forget the day to day details. In some ways that's good, kind of. But it can be dangerous to forget–especially, if we get complacent. I know everything could change in an instant.

Addiction statistics are depressing. Only 10% of people seek treatment. And only 10% of those find lasting recovery. I hope for a world where the deck isn't so stacked against humanity. Because in the end, despite living a life beyond our wildest, a life full of miracles that just a short time ago never felt possible, it still feels sometimes as if we're just cheating death. Or relapse. Sometimes, they don't feel that different, and too often, they are one in the same.

I'm immensely proud of the work Scott has done, and that I have done, and that Ara has done. I hope we wear our battle scars well and our journey continues to help other people. It's the most we can wish for, and, with every ounce of my being, I hope we're not wishing for too much.

CHAPTER 37

Scott

The one thing that has helped me get over the hump of not drinking in social situations is to make the first comment about why I'm not drinking or about my rehab experience. I might say I had to retire my drinking shoes. Or I'll just flat out say that I'm an alcoholic. I want to soften the stigma about rehab and let people know that I don't have a problem talking about it. So, if *they* want to talk about my addiction, then do it to my face, not behind my back. And, I know a lot of the recovery community is based on anonymity, but not only do I talk about my recovery openly, but I want my wife to talk about my addiction and recovery, as well. And hers. I'm not saying that I would break any confidences when it came to others' recoveries, I'm just saying that for me, things go much better when I'm open about it.

When anyone walks into my office at Argo now, they see my certificates of completion from both BHOPB and Kolmac framed and hanging on the wall. Before, I had always been proud of my drinking. Now, I am proud that I completed something. Treatment is a very important part of what I have done and who I have become. I figure it is harder for people to talk shit about something you are proud of doing. I also hope my openness will lead others to get help.

Most of the employees I had when I was a raging alcoholic and drug addict have moved on. Only a few really know my journey, how much I have changed and what I was like to work for before I went into treatment.

Now, most of Argo's staff just know me as the crazy boss who's always going into his office to meditate. They know me for the wild stories I sometimes tell about my previous life. They know me as the person who openly admits to being an alcoholic and a druggie. They know that no good ever came, or will ever come, from my drinking. They hear stories about me when they go out to some of the other establishments on our little drag.

But what matters to me most is what they *don't* know me for. They don't know me as the boss who would tell them they weren't allowed to drink on the job, and then would do shots in front of them. They don't know me as the boss who, in order to drink some more, would ask them to call me when I was at home and give some fake reason I needed to come back to work. They don't know me for the rage I had when something didn't go the way I thought it should. They don't know me as the person who trusted no one.

My employees might actually like me now—though that may be stretching it. But I am certainly a much better and easier person to work for. Of course, the "bar" (no pun intended) had been set pretty low to begin with. Because Shaaren and I work together and because addiction affects everybody in its path, we can see our own health reflected in the high quality staff that we have now.

I have learned so much. I have grown more in these last couple years of being in recovery than I did in the almost twenty years I spent using drugs and alcohol. I can honestly say that, for the first time in my life since I was a little kid, I am experiencing real happiness.

On vacation in Massachusetts, August 10, 2012

It has been a long and painful journey. But I am incredibly grateful for it.

Now, in my mid-thirties, I feel I have a second chance at life. A life that I never thought possible. I am blessed with a beautiful family, a thriving business, and a healthy life both physically and mentally. But that healthy life takes work. I still attend a continuing care outpatient treatment program once a week at the Kolmac Clinic. That keeps me focused. And because of that, I can walk past the Argonaut's two bars and rooms full of alcohol on the way to my office.

I'm certainly not going to say that I don't still think about drinking sometimes. But I don't think about drinking all the time anymore. I still have good and bad days, but the bad days are fewer and farther between.

And memories help keep me sober too. I have seen so many people in the restaurant industry fall to drugs and alcohol. I have looked in the mirror often enough and seen the pain in my own eyes. And I've seen the same pain in the eyes of so many people in the restaurant world. That world has its own rules. It drew us in because of the lifestyle it offered—the never-ending party—only to cause us so much pain and close us off from the larger world. I always thought everyone drank like me. I thought everyone used cocaine and pot. As it turns out, not really.

Now, working once again in a restaurant on a street that keeps adding new bars and restaurants, I am constantly reminded of just how powerful the pull of this world and my disease is. I've marked the continuing deaths of young people. I've seen people fall off the wagon after ten or twenty years of sobriety. And I've watched as they destroy everything and everyone around them in the process. I am so familiar with that same destruction. And I know it could still happen to me at any time. That knowledge was confirmed by my two relapses. I know I have to watch my back for the rest of my life. But I've also come to realize that a healthy life has so much more to offer. And I believe I can live that healthy life and still run a restaurant and bar.

I also know that my wife lives with the fear that one day I might give in to temptation and think I can handle alcohol or drugs again. It's the fear of everyone who loves an addict. For the addict, using again might lead to death, but for loved ones, the pain caused by the addict is much greater than death. They must live with the destruction, the questions, the feelings of shame and guilt. They have to carry that for the rest of their lives. Addiction destroys so many lives. In some ways, the addict has it easy and can take the easy way out. The family of the addict feels most of the pain.

I hope my daughter will not remember me as a drinker and drug user. But she will know about it. After all, she is being raised in a recovering home. I hope that knowing the truth and realities of addiction will give her the tools to make smart, educated decisions for herself when she is older.

I rate my decision to go to Kolmac for outpatient treatment as the third best one in my life. It comes right behind marrying my wife and going to inpatient treatment. If I had not continued my treatment, I am 100 percent sure that I would not be sober today. Maybe those arm-twisters along the way really did know a thing or two.

If I hadn't met Shaaren, I probably wouldn't be here at all. She helped save my life. More than anyone else, she made me the person I am now. Although I didn't always like it at the time, she was constantly pushing me to be better and kinder. To be a better father, husband, and boss. I'm positive that I am a better person because of my wife. Once I got sober, I could see that my path of self-destruction would have led me to the grave if it wasn't for her. As they say, behind every great man is a better woman. I can finally see how lucky I am to have such a strong person in my life.

Do I regret my past? Do I regret my drinking and my drug use? I do regret not stopping earlier. I regret the pain I caused. I regret not being there for my mother and the pain I've inflicted on my wife and daughter.

I don't regret it all, though. I have stories that would horrify many, but they still make me laugh. My life has brought me to this point. All of this makes me who I am. If my story can help even one person, it will be worth it. And if I can lead by example in the restaurant industry, if I can be living proof that people can change *and* that change can be good, it will be worth it. I want people to know that it is possible to have a rewarding career in the hospitality industry without the use of drugs and alcohol. I want them to know that it's possible to be in this profession without getting sucked into its darker side. I want them to know that even if you are sucked in, there is a way out.

My name is Scott Magnuson and I am a recovering alcoholic and drug addict.

i   Lit. My car was in the front yard, I came in through the window, sleeping with my clothes on. "My Own Worst Enemy." A Place in the Sun. CD. RCA. 1999.

ii   Hahn, F. (2005, August 26) Plans to Set the Bar High on H Street NE *The Washington Post* Retrieved from http://www.washingtonpost.com/

iii   Meditate and Destroy. Dir. Sarah Fisher. Kino Lorber Films. 2009

iv   Levine, Noah. *Dharma Punx: A Memoir.* New York: HarperCollins Publishers, 2009. Print.